RIPPLES
FROM PEACE LAKE

————

Essays for Mediators and Peacemakers

————

ERIC R. GALTON

TRAFFORD

• Canada • UK • Ireland • USA •

Note for Librarians: a cataloguing record for this book that includes Dewey Decimal Classification and US Library of Congress numbers is available from the Library and Archives of Canada. The complete cataloguing record can be obtained from their online database at:
www.collectionscanada.ca/amicus/index-e.html
ISBN 1-4120-4638-6

TRAFFORD

Offices in Canada, USA, Ireland, UK and Spain
This book was published *on-demand* in cooperation with Trafford Publishing. On-demand publishing is a unique process and service of making a book available for retail sale to the public taking advantage of on-demand manufacturing and Internet marketing. On-demand publishing includes promotions, retail sales, manufacturing, order fulfilment, accounting and collecting royalties on behalf of the author.

Book sales for North America and international:
Trafford Publishing, 6E–2333 Government St.,
Victoria, BC v8t 4p4 CANADA
phone 250 383 6864 (toll-free 1 888 232 4444)
fax 250 383 6804; email to orders@trafford.com
Book sales in Europe:
Trafford Publishing (uk) Ltd., Enterprise House,
Wistaston Road Business Centre, Wistaston Road, Crewe,
Cheshire cw2 7rp UNITED KINGDOM
phone 01270 251 396 (local rate 0845 230 9601)
facsimile 01270 254 983; orders.uk@trafford.com
Order online at:
www.trafford.com/robots/04-2446.html

10 9 8 7 6 5 4 3 2

Two roads diverged in a wood, and I –
I took the one less traveled by,
and that has made all the difference.
The Road Not Taken, Robert Frost

For all mediators and peacemakers
who follow the less traveled road
and for my peacemakers,
Kim, Katie, Kaela, Justin, Seth, and Noah

Acknowledgements

I would like to express my deep appreciation to those who helped me with this book or who have inspired me.

I would first express my gratitude, admiration, respect, and love for my wife Kimberlee Kovach. Professor Kovach has been a beacon of light and a leader in the alternative dispute resolution movement and has inspired so many with her writing, teaching, and training. Kim also keeps me honest and has profoundly shaped my views and thoughts about mediation. Thank you Kim for showing me the way.

I would also like to especially thank my colleagues and dear friends at the Lakeside Mediation Center for their guidance, inspiration, support, and friendship. My "brothers," Ben Cunningham and Greg Bourgeois have inspired me by being fantastic mediators and also by being there for me always. Pat Hazel, Joe Hart, David Moore and Bert Pluymen, my other Lakesiders, have become dear and valued friends. Special thanks to Greg for telling me to keep writing at a moment when I was ready to quit.

Thank you as well to Jeff Kichaven a/k/a Cuz, for writing such excellent articles, being such an amazing mediator, and an especially good friend. Ditto to my other cousin, Avi Schneebalg, the founding father of Belgian mediation.

As always, deep thanks to the founding father of mediation in Texas, the Honorable Frank Evans, who shaped my decision to be a mediator, and the Honorable Joe Hart, who allowed me to chair our first settlement week and actually mediate my first cases.

Special thanks to Andrea Tuck for translating what I wrote on yellow pads.

Thanks also to my children, Justin, Seth, Noah, Kaela & Katie for being my constant sources of joy and pride and for putting up with my incessant mediation travels.

Thanks also to all the mediators and trainers who I have had the pleasure to meet and work with over the years.

Also, thanks to the disputants who have both inspired and taught me.

Finally, thanks to Peace Lake for just being there. By sun or moon, she is ever beautiful and I feel traces of her magic in my heart and in my soul.

Table of Contents

Introduction

Greetings fellow mediators and peacemakers. I've been wanting to write to you for quite a long time.

My last books, <u>Mediation: A Texas Practice Guide</u>, and <u>Representing Clients in Mediation</u> were published in 1991. I did not feel any compulsion to write second editions of those books, even though they received very kind reviews. I have never written simply just to write. I went back to doing what I know and love and do four or five times a week; namely, mediating disputes.

Today, something over 3,100 mediations later, I love my work more than when I first began. I am in awe of the mediation process and my passion and respect for mediation has grown over time. I really cannot imagine doing anything else, and cannot think of anything else, especially in today's world, that is more constructive and socially valuable. Being a mediator is an honor and privilege.

With time, my respect, admiration, and affection for mediators and peacemakers has only deepened. I also have profound admiration and appreciation for the dispute resolution scholars who have inspired us and motivated us to become better at what we do.

I wrote <u>Ripples</u> for two reasons. First I wanted

to write something to honor, recognize, and hopefully inspire my dear colleagues who labor in the trenches helping people resolve terrible and dire disputes. I wanted to write about things that you, my colleagues, may not have read before but you will intuitively understand. If any of these essays provide new insight and skills for my colleagues, which I hope many of them will do, then this work will not be in vain. I also wrote essays that I very much hope will inspire you, especially during the lonely moments you walk down those inevitable dark paths. In my most hopeful moments, I wanted to touch the souls of my fellow peacemakers. I hope that one or more of these essays will make you smile or move you in some way.

As is my custom, I did not attempt to write treatises on any of these topics. In fact I took the opposite approach. Given the busy compressed lives of neutrals, I wanted to offer you some of my best thoughts which you could read easily and very quickly. I had more to write on each topic; but, that may come later. I thought that certain essays would resonate on different levels to a wonderfully diverse audience. Also, I was hoping to write the mediator's equivalent of golf's <u>Little Red Book</u>; something not terribly large that my friends could carry with them and read at moments of maximum desperation.

I also was motivated to write <u>Ripples</u> because of the troubled times in which we live. I will admit freely I am a "cup half full" person and by nature, an optimist, and hopeful. I have lived through the duck and cover drills, race riots, and Vietnam; but, I have never felt more uncertain about the state of the world than I do today.

The violence and conflicts which rage in our world are horrifying to all people of good heart. But, I think the escalating cycle of conflict has to be especially appalling to mediators and peacemakers. When I begin my law school mediation class, I always tell my students that we have no shortage of warriors in this world and that I am recruiting them to the order of peacemakers. At no time in modern history are peacemakers more needed. We need to broaden our professional view and begin to see ourselves as part of the solution to a violent world and a world in conflict. What skills we have acquired and what we have learned may have an even higher calling. We may not rest until we live in a world which respects nonviolence and diversity and which values peacemaking more than the terrible tools of war. One essay in Ripples is my stream of conscience recollection of September 11 as it played out on the deck by my mediation center. Please forgive the indulgence; but, Ripples would be less than complete if I did not share those feelings with you.

I remain hopeful and believe we can and do make a difference. You provide the blessing of peace every time you roll up your sleeves and assist people on that difficult journey.

I wrote much of this work by Lake Austin, which flows by our Lakeside Mediation Center. On September 11, I renewed my commitment to call her Peace Lake because she sustained me then and has inspired me many times since. I draw strength from her waters and it is the place that I find peace when I need it.

This book is like the stones I often throw into Peace Lake, sometimes to the consternation of the channel catfish and turtles. I watch the ripples go out and for some reason it provides me with hope and a sense of a larger purpose.

These essays are like my stones. Where they will go and who they will reach is unknown to me. But, I do have faith and hope that they will mean something to you and will do some good.

In the end, we must believe. We must always have hope.

Eric Galton
Austin, Texas
August, 2004

Chapter 1

The Art of Mediation

In the hour before a mediation, I sometimes visualize a blank canvas. Today, I am an artist and I see a canvas that is white, pristine and waiting for me.

The blank canvas means many things to me. Visualizing a blank canvas compels me to banish any preconceptions, judgments, prejudices or thoughts as to what will happen. I purposely forget what the parties or lawyers have sent me to read in advance. I lose any thought of what the people might look like or how they might behave.

The blank canvas also symbolizes opportunity. I become energized by the feeling that by day's end the canvas will look entirely different.

The blank canvas also demands creativity. What will be painted is entirely unknown. What colors or tones will appear is uncertain. The only thing I do know with certainty is that the canvas will be unique and different from any other.

I also know one other thing. I will not be painting today to please myself. The painting will not be what I want to create. The painting, when it is done, will be created by others. I will supply the brush, the paint, and my hand and they will supply the inspiration and direction. I must be willing to lose control. I also should not worry about the preliminary outline which will appear because the painting will go in directions that I cannot predict. In the end, the painting will belong to them. I will try to bring life, color, and structure to their vision.

But, some of me will also make its way onto the canvas. I will know when the tone is too muted and provide the suggestion of bright colors. I will sense when the picture is becoming too real and subtly change to the more abstract. I will create a mood which allows the painting to be completed. To motivate change, one must be a chameleon. Like a chameleon, I will adjust my colors and adapt. I will be very present but almost undetected.

So few of these moments are conscious or the product of objective thought. The softer strokes and the occasional splashes of color are in essence the mediator as an artist- an artist who assists others in creating a painting they never visualized or imagined before.

Sometimes, on other mornings, I feel like a jazz musician. I am the drummer who is playing with musicians I have not met before and who do not truly know each other.

Dave, on the electric guitar, is powerful and very,

very fast. His fingers fly over the frets weaving in one direction and then another. Lisa, on the bass, is more structured and more disciplined. Lisa wants to develop the context of Dave's riffs, to hear them realized; but, Dave veers away any time anyone gets close to catching up. Sam, on saxophone, seems subdued; waiting for the moment his instrument may truly give song. Sam seems willing to let Dave push him in different directions; but, he doesn't know how to push back. Kara, on keyboards, is able to insinuate a line to move the music somewhere else. Kara's fingers seem to go faster with each of Dave's riffs.

I'm in the background, surrounded by my drums. My art is to somehow figure out each of these interesting and talented musicians and establish a beat that each musician can live with. I relish their diversity and I honor each musician's skill. But, the beat I will create today will reconcile their differences and allow their amazing individual talents to take a different, more unique form. That is my art. I am content to be in the background, changing the beat, and allowing my bandmates to make wonderful music which will surprise them. There's a trick to this art, you know. You move them without any of them knowing you are. When the set is over, each of them will seem almost shocked that it happened and that things worked. They don't know why. But, the drummer always knows.

This afternoon, I am a director encouraging the actors to improvise and move away from the same script. The actors seem stuck, unenthusiastic, and uninspired. Each of the actors seems to be wearing a mask and pretending to be engaged in the moment. They speak their lines in a way they think they should be said instead of how they really feel it. With the male lead, my attempts at being more subdued and suggestive have failed. He needs a director who will turn up the volume. I also made a mistake with the lead actress. I thought she had invited me to be very direct and specific. But, she didn't mean it. I was a little too honest this morning. I have to make amends with her and try a different approach.

Sometimes, I wish I had someone to talk to when things are going poorly; but, most of the time, I'm glad I don't. There is an element of danger and drama behind the scenes. Just at the veritable brink of the cliff, some hero surfaces and saves the day. That's the interesting bit. A hero is almost always lurking around somewhere if I'm just not so blind that I can't find her. This art, or so I have learned it, is a form of second sight, another sense. It's what happens when the lights go out and you lose your vision. I imagine it's like an unfamiliar room suddenly going pitch black. There's a door to this room somewhere. Somehow you have to find it.

These feelings on different mornings, the painter, the musician, the director, speak to me about the art of mediation. The art is the inexact science of it, the mystery of the process, and the qualities of the process that make it virtually indefinable. The art of the mediator is to paint almost invisibly, play a beat that will work but no one will notice, or to direct in such a way that heroes are born. Unlike an artist, you never get to show your work and because you were in the background your work may also be forgotten. But, the disappearing nature of your craft is part of the art as well.

Chapter 2

On Trust Building

"It's a matter of trust."
Billy Joel, A Matter of Trust

Who is a mediator when he walks into a room of disputants for the first time? Simply put, a mediator is almost always a complete, total stranger to the parties.

Of course, the parties may have well read a biography furnished by the mediator, and if they are represented, been advised about the mediator by counsel. But, regardless, the mediator remains a stranger who is about to become involved in perhaps the most significant problem affecting the parties' lives.

Why should the parties, therefore, trust the mediator; or, for that matter, a process that is unfamiliar or new to them? Often, the parties are not at their best at this moment. Parties are frequently apprehensive, mistrusting, nervous, skeptical, unhappy, depressed, physically ill, or maybe just frightened.

Also, people may find themselves in the physical presence of someone they believe may have harmed them, either physically, emotionally, or financially. While all mediations do not have these ingredients, many mediations do. The tension is real and palpable. The parties are feeling these things. And, the mediator feels it. How does the mediator develop trust and in what ways is trust built?

I would like to approach this matter chronologically. What may mediators do to develop trust before the parties arrive and what may mediators do to develop trust during the mediation session?

The initial question involves a reality check by the mediator herself. The mediator must appreciate the huge leap of faith she is requesting the parties to make by buying into the process and trusting the mediator. Mediation is not therapy; but, mental health professionals often require months with a patient before he "opens up." Business relationships are often cultured over months, if not years. Personal relationships and friendships involve time. The mediator-disputant relationship must be developed very quickly. Many disputants will necessarily rely on first impressions and ask, "Is this a person whom I may trust?"

What makes you trust a stranger in very difficult, trying circumstances? Imagine the following. You are out of town on business and you receive a call informing you that your mother, unexpectedly, is in the hospital and critically ill. You need to get to the hospital immediately. You rush to the airport, impatiently wait in line, and are now standing in front of the reservationists for the airline. You realize you will have to disclose some very personal information to this stranger in order to explain your urgent need. In this moment of crisis what may this stranger do to earn your trust? Also, visualize how quickly you are forming an opinion of this reservationist. You will decide quickly whether he is someone you may trust. Similar situations might involve taking your sick child to the pediatrician while on family vacation or going to the bank when you discover your wallet has been stolen while on a business trip.

In each instance, you need help. In each instance, you must disclose personal information. In each instance, time is precious. In each instance, you are anxious and concerned. In each instance, you are relying on a professional you don't know to do something important. In each instance, you are forming an almost instantaneous impression of whether you trust this person to help you in a very important situation.

If you are visualizing how you might feel in any of these circumstances, you are now in the proper mental state of assessing how disputants may be reacting to you.

Before the mediation itself, you may be in the preliminary stages of trust building.

The obvious first step is to assess what you publish about yourself and what information you have on your website. Many mediators view web sites from a marketing perspective. In this instance, focus on what you publish or say from a trust building perspective.

I believe a critical element of trust building involves making the mediator accessible as a human being from the parties' perspectives. Education, training, length of service as a mediator, number of mediations, accreditations may well validate a mediator and fill a portion of a party's trust needs. People do respond to and trust people who are serious about their work and accomplished in their chosen career. But, such information only tells part of the story and does not fully make the mediator accessible or lead to trust. Parties are often looking for the "people things" that make the mediator accessible and approachable.

Many people form visual impressions and may be wondering, "What does the mediator look like?" Does the mediator appear warm, friendly and open?

Many people respond to family. Does the mediator have a spouse, children, grandchildren, nephews or nieces? Mediators and parties often need something else to talk about in tense moments or long waits during mediation. Many people like to talk about their children and find such discussions calming.

A mediator might also identify hobbies or activities as a method of creating accessibility. A mediator might have a passion for whitewater rafting, writing or may do volunteer work for the elderly. Disputants actually read these things with the same enthusiasm as they do your description of the mediation process. A disputant might have a charitable program he is very involved in and your disclosure might open up a door to such discussion.

Another facet of advance trust building is to underscore your commitment to core principles of mediation. Neutrality, as we'll discuss later, is not a natural state of being for most people. People are not, by nature, neutral and are rarely exposed to people who are. You might want to explain neutrality, why it is so important to the process, and your unswerving commitment to neutrality. Such a message is both educational, reassuring, and builds trust.

Similarly, you might also discuss confidentiality, its importance, and your commitment to confidentiality. You may be thinking that people inherently understand or trust your proclamation of confidentiality. You are probably wrong. In a recent mediation in a private caucus, a woman in her sixties advised me that she had no belief that any one could be neutral or keep matters confidential. Most people, out of a sense of politeness or fear, would not have said such a thing so openly. But, I was delighted with her honesty and viewed her statement as a real way of building trust. The women anticipated that I would become defensive or upset. After I thanked her for her honest expression of concern, we had a wonderful chat about neutrality and it became a bridge to trust.

As you understand, you may only go so far in developing trust before the mediation because trust is inherently interpersonal, visceral, and often an earned feeling. Assuming your prior disclosures have been reassuring and have created the seedlings of trust, how does one nurture and help those seedlings to grow?

We will discuss at length in another essay the mediation environment; but, for now, the trust building process continues the moment the disputants walk in to your office. How do people feel when they walk into your mediation office or center? Do you know? What are you trying to communicate? Whether you know it or not, you are communicating something. For purposes of this section on trust building, analyze whether your office environment helps build trust.

The first point of direct contact with the mediator is usually the mediation coordinator or receptionist. People form instantaneous reactions regarding this person, which has a great deal to do with trust.

People trust preparedness and professionalism.

If the coordinator acts like he is expecting the party and knows where to place the party, the party feels more confident. The coordinator must be warm, "a people person," and should make the party feel welcome and comfortable. The coordinator should meet any immediate need of the party. Is coffee or water available? Where are the restrooms?

And, the coordinator should know something about mediation. I would recommend that any coordinator or receptionist take the 40-hour basic mediation training. The coordinator must be acutely aware that emotions may be running high and that parties are apprehensive and tense. A negative impression at the initial point of contact may erode any trust that has been built previously. An indifferent, aloof, unprepared coordinator will signal the opposite of professionalism and possibly enhance the parties' apprehension.

Where should the mediator be as the parties arrive? I think there are two schools of thought on this question. One view is that the mediator should cloister himself away until all the parties arrive, to avoid any other party misconstruing the greeting or viewing it as an absence of neutrality. This writer believes in the second view, which is that such a greeting enhances trust and that the dangers of misconstruing hospitality are slight. The parties should be made to feel welcome. The parties should appreciate that the mediator is prepared and ready to proceed.

Some attention to trust building has been focused on the mediator's introduction during the initial joint session; but, we also understand that trust building occurs both before and after the mediator's introduction.

As we know, the mediator's introduction has many purposes and many goals. One goal of the mediator's introduction is to establish trust. How does one meet that goal effectively?

Much time has been spent in training and the literature on the contents or the elements of the mediator's introduction. And, some debate the length of the mediator's introduction. Some believe the introduction should be between five to ten minutes. Others believe the introduction should be between twenty to thirty minutes. I would like to solely focus on content as it relates to trust building.

Preliminarily, the mediator should not assume the parties have read or understood what has been communicated about the process before the mediation. If the parties are represented by counsel, one must consider what the lawyer may have told them about the mediation process and the mediator's role. For example, a lawyer might have advised his client "you may never trust any mediator." Or, a lawyer may have advised her client "you may trust the mediator completely." And, to make this even more challenging, the client may not even trust his own lawyer.

The preparedness of your mediator's introduction establishes trust. Preparedness does not mean scripted. But, a mediator's introduction delivered without notes, which is complete, and correctly delivered, enhances trust.

Some have suggested that the mediator's introduction is an opportunity to make new friends. Perhaps, the introduction is an opportunity to develop trust. The tone of the introduction should be enthusiastic and evidence commitment to the process and the parties. Eye contact is essential and should be balanced.

The background or qualifications section of the introduction should be sufficient enough to establish confidence without betraying humility. Qualifications, education and commitment to the process establish trust. The qualifications section should include brief personal information; again, the human piece that makes the mediator more accessible and humanizes the mediator.

I think neutrality and confidentiality are usually referenced by the mediator as part of her introduction, with inadequate attention to what these concepts mean and the mediator's commitment to them. As stated, neutrality and confidentiality are not everyday commodities; but, these core elements of the process are the foundations of trust. A mediator that simply states, "I pledge to be neutral and preserve the confidentiality of the process" has explained nothing and done little to establish trust.

At the very least, a mediator should explain briefly what neutrality means. But, understanding that parties may be cynical or view the neutral state to be unnatural, the mediator might also acknowledge that the parties may have such feelings and explain why neutrality is critical to the process and so important ethically and professionally to the mediator. The same approach would apply to confidentiality. In total, the expanded version of neutrality and confidentiality might take just a few extra minutes. But, in terms of trust building, the effort may yield great dividends.

The description of how the mediation will unfold also enhances trust. People are more confident about and trust a process they come to understand. People like to know "where they are" and "what is going to happen next."

Finally, and as part of the mediator's introduction, the mediator must establish his belief in the process and his belief in the power of the parties. Parties may not yet trust the process completely; but it helps the parties' levels of trust to know the mediator is confident.

The mediator's introduction, if done incorrectly or poorly, may damage trust. Because mediation is a flexible process, absolute rules rarely exist; but in terms of trust building during the introduction, you might consider the following issues.

Never promise what you can't deliver, and never, more pointedly, promise happiness. The easiest way to damage trust is to make a promise that you cannot obviously keep. While happiness, for example, is always a good thing, resolution does not always involve happiness. Do not promise a result or guaranty when the process will end. The only promises you can keep are your effort, attention, commitment, neutrality, and confidentiality.

Never suggest you can walk in a party's shoes if you have not been in a similar situation. You don't know what it is like to lose a child if you have not in fact lost a child. To suggest otherwise erodes confidence and trust.

Never promise to listen and then not listen. You tell a party you will sincerely listen to his opening statement and then appear disinterested and inattentive. If so, trust is gone, perhaps irretrievably.

Never promise that you will be non judgmental and then be obviously judgmental. Cutting off a party because you are disinterested feels judgmental. Rolling your eyes or shuffling your paper hurts. And, any promise you don't keep damages trust.

The inverse, of course, is that keeping your promises establishes and enhances trust. A party who believes the mediator really listened is likely to trust the mediator and the process. A party who feels that the mediator is really being patient is likely to trust the mediator and the process. Simply, keeping promises establishes trust.

In this sense trust building occurs throughout the process and may be enhanced or lost at any time. The commitment to listen is a commitment to listen <u>throughout</u> the process. The mediator's commitment to patience is a <u>process wide</u> commitment. And, a mediator's commitment to be the last person to give up is observed and measured <u>throughout</u> the process. Finally the parties are continuously monitoring and evaluating your commitment to neutrality and confidentiality throughout the process.

Parties need a process they may trust and a mediator they trust to participate meaningfully in the process and for mediation to work its magic. The mediator should be constantly attempting to develop and build trust.

Mediators, in advanced training courses, often want to learn techniques that will help break impasses. Many effective techniques exist in this regard; but, none of these techniques will work consistently unless and until the mediator builds trust with the parties.

Chapter 3

On Private Caucus

"If I had ever been here before
I would probably know just what to do."
DeJa Vu, Crosby, Stills, Nash & Young

While much has been written regarding whether to use the private caucus, little has been written on what to do in a private caucus. I will leave it to others to debate the appropriateness of the private caucus and discuss instead the purpose of the private caucus and techniques that seem to enhance its value.

Trust building runs through the mediation process like a river. The first private caucus is the most intimate, direct interaction between the mediator and a party. Hopefully the mediator's introduction and the mediation environment have begun the process of trust building. But, trust has likely not been established fully by the first private caucus and a party may have no idea or the wrong idea of what to expect from the mediator in this new situation.

The most comon misconception, usually related by the party's lawyer, is that the mediator "beats both sides up" in private caucus. I have actually heard lawyers say these words to their clients. In such instances, the party may be expecting a cross-examination or worse. As such, the party's guard is up and the party may be apprehensive, fearful, and defensive.

Most of the time a party has no real idea what to expect in the first private caucus. A mediator may have briefly described caucus in his introduction, but the party may not have heard or fully understand it. In such instances, a party may be somewhat trusting but nervous simply because he does not really know what will happen next.

In the first caucus, a mediator has several goals. First, the mediator should continue the trust building process. Second, the mediator needs to obtain a great deal of information, especially about the party's needs and interests. Third, the mediator needs to understand where, if anywhere, negotiations stand. Because of the need to meet important goals and especially to establish trust, reality testing should not begin in earnest during the first caucus, if it even begins at all.

Trust building in caucus is firmly established if the mediator occupies primarily a listening role and avoids the temptation to barrage the party with questions or overwhelm a party. To be a good listener, a mediator has to be a good questioner. Asking questions well also serves to meet the second goal; i.e., obtaining information and understanding needs and interests.

When I walk in to the first private caucus, I want to sit next to or close to the party. Sitting across the table creates a barrier. Four lawyers between the mediator and the party is a barrier.

Next, you probably have a note pad with you; but resist the temptation to take notes during the first private caucus. If you feel compelled to take notes, take precious few. Note taking interferes with your true goals; may impede trust building, and is often a useless exercise (You never read many of these notes). If you tend to be obsessive, you may always jot a few notes down after you leave. The first private caucus should have the feel of a conversation in your den- not an interview or a cross-examination.

A good approach after you enter the room is to say nothing for ten seconds. Some mediators feel the need to ask questions constantly and do most of the talking. The reason you wait ten seconds is that at least half the time the party will begin speaking before you even ask a question.

If the party begins speaking, listen; Do not interrupt! Do not feel compelled to ask a question! Do not try to redirect the conversation. The party is trying to steer you where he needs to go. Trust building involves allowing the party to set his own agenda.

Also, a party usually begins speaking about something that is very important to him. Some people have unique rituals about having an important discussion. A party may have to discuss an entirely unrelated matter as a prelude to what is truly important.

Additionally, you will likely get more information by simply listening than from any questions you might ask. Finally, interruption seems judgmental. Many people feel they have not had a full and complete opportunity to tell their story, their way, and in their own time.

Often, a party may remain silent after your ten seconds of silence are over. The party may not know what to say. The party may be apprehensive. Or, the party may be simply deferential to your role and expecting you to ask the first question. Your first question in the first caucus is probably the most important question you will ask. If you have read the essay On Spacing, you have given yourself ten or fifteen minutes after the joint session to think. One of the things you should be thinking about is, "What is the first question I am going to ask each party?" Spacing allows for analysis and restraint. Restraint means not asking the five or ten specific questions you are dying to ask. You will get to ask these questions, however, these questions will not be your first question.

Basic mediation training focuses on the value of

open-ended questions for a reason. Open-ended questions provide the party with an avenue to give the mediator a great deal of information.

But, I believe there are two types of open-ended questions; namely, informational open-ended questions and feelings open-ended questions.

An informational open-ended question might be "Why do you think Bill intended to hurt you?" Technically, this question is an open-ended question. But, an informational open-ended question is intended to generate factual information. Informational open-ended questions are very important; but, such questions should not be your first question. Why not? Such questions put the discussion on a factual track. Also, such questions do little to help establish trust. Finally such questions do not help identify a party's underlying interests and needs.

Your first question should be a feelings open-ended question. A feelings question shifts the agenda outside the box of facts and positions towards a different world involving needs, emotions, and interests.

You may create literally thousands of feelings open-ended questions. Permit me to provide a few illustrations.

"Bill, I can tell you are very disappointed with Sam. Help me better understand your disappointment and what disappoints you the most."

"Jane, I noticed when Ron's lawyer was speaking

you became very angry. What was going through your mind at that moment and what was making you so upset?"

"John, I know this hurts a lot. Help me understand how all this is affecting you and what hurts the most?"

At the risk of being repetitive, you must actually listen after you ask such a question. You must resist the temptation to interrupt. You must discipline yourself not to even think about your next question. The response to such a question is the true beginning of the journey. Many people don't expect you to listen. Many people expect to be judged. Many people expect you to be disinterested. Many people do not expect you to be empathetic. But, you listen patiently, empathetically and nonjudgmentally. You will be creating the sacred world of trust and the special world that mediation offers to people in crisis. A party will say to you at some time during the process, "You were the first person who really listened and understood."

Another first caucus mistake is to jump shift feelings to facts. You asked a wonderful feelings open-ended question. The party responded. Then you ask, "Was anyone in the car wearing seatbelts?"

Fact oriented questions immediately after important feelings questions may take the air out of the balloon and damage trust. In this regard, you have several options. You may not need at all to get into the facts during the first caucus. Or, after a party is through expressing deep feeling, you might ask a transition question. A transition question is purposely non-specific. An illustration of a transition question is as follows.

"Steve, I really appreciate your helping me better understand how you feel. Help me better understand what this dispute is really about."

A good transition question allows the party to identify and organize facts. Equally important, the party usually begins with the facts that are most important to him. Transitions questions are not threatening and do not adversely impact the trust building process.

Does the mediator always want to come out of the first caucus with a proposal? The only answer to this question is "it depends." A mediator just has to trust his sense of feel on this issue. The first caucus may have been so emotional and effective that the mediator might elect to let that moment sink in before moving to negotiations. On the other hand, the mediator might sense the parties wish for things to be in motion quickly and move to the negotiation phase.

If your gut tells you proposals should begin, you might consider this the perfect time for a space and perhaps helping the parties understand another of your many roles.

As for the space, you want the party to have some

private time to consider what proposal he is willing to make. Excellent mediators know when to excuse themselves from the room.

At the same time, you want the party to understand his task and also understand how you may be helpful in the negotiation process. I'd offer the following illustration in this regard.

"Sarah, thank you for helping me understand this better. I get the feeling you want to begin the negotiations to try and resolve this dispute. I am going to give you ten or fifteen minutes on your own to think about what your first proposal might be. One way of looking at what I do is to serve as the traffic cop of the negotiations. However, I am not here to tell you what to do or to tell James what to do. I can, after you formulate a proposal, provide you with input regarding whether a proposal will be helpful. You will always make the final decision and you are not obliged to follow any input I give you. This is your negotiation and that is why, after such a helpful discussion, I want to give you time to think about what would be a good first proposal."

I think mediators may create a theme of the mediator being a helper and assistant to the negotiations. A mediator's input is never telling the party what to do; but, rather asking questions about a proposal that allows the party to self-evaluate. Consider the following questions.

"Sarah, if your proposal was being made to you, how would you react to it?"

"Sarah, how do you expect James will react to your proposal?"

"Sarah, is there a way to reframe your proposal so that it gets a more positive reception?"

Another thing the mediator must remain acutely aware of during the caucus phase is how long she has left the other party alone. Mediators lose track of time because of the necessarily intense focus. But, a mediator should be vigilant never to leave a party alone for too long.

You are now, after a five-minute space, about to begin your first caucus with the other party. Assume you also have a proposal in your back pocket.

Never (I realize there are a few "nevers" and "always" in mediations) begin your first caucus with the other side's proposal. Everything you did in your other first caucus you need to do with this party in order to establish trust, to understand needs and interests, and to cement the relationship. Once you submit a proposal, a party will think about nothing else. The submission of the first proposal occurs at the end of your first caucus with the other party.

Experienced mediators know when they are carrying a constructive first proposal or a possibly destructive one. Many parties have been conditioned to expect an unreasonable first proposal and mediators constantly manage such disappointment by reassuring parties that negotiation is a process and it only matters where things end and not where they begin. But, what if the first proposal is both credible and constructive?

I have heard and read experts opine, both favorably and unfavorably, about manipulation in mediation. I think some manipulation by the mediator, if it is not heavy handed, is inevitable. Let's return to that good first proposal in your back pocket. You might consider asking the following question.

"You know, James, Sara gave me an initial proposal to submit to you. What do you think her proposal is?"

Because parties often expect the worst, a party, far more often than not, will describe a proposal that is much worse than the proposal you are carrying. If so, you have a wonderful opportunity to place the negotiations on a very good track. You might say something like this to James.

"You know, Sarah's proposal is much more reasonable than what you just described. Let me tell you what it is. I think when you hear her proposal you will feel we are already making very good progress and this process is working."

Constructive initial caucuses set the tone for the many caucuses which will follow. One final thought about caucuses. Once you have separated the parties, the parties do not have to stay separate and if the situation warrants you may elect to bring them back together. Consider the essay <u>On People Moving.</u>

Good caucus technique helps resolve many disputes. The feel does not have to evolve into the "beating up" that many people think will happen. And, mediation should never involve "beating" up anyone. Bludgeoning is the evidence of lack of technique and is entirely inconsistent with the mediation paradigm.

Chapter 4

On Timing

"In all this talk of time, talk is fine"
The Great Beyond, REM

Timing is of the most important attributes of a successful mediator or peacemaker. "Timing" is the <u>when</u> to do something in the process. Timing is rarely discussed and almost never taught. I wonder whether timing is a teachable skill at all or whether it is purely instinctive. But, every outstanding mediator possesses remarkable timing. The purpose of this essay is to attempt to at least be aware of timing and get our arms around the concept. But, simply stated, <u>when</u> you do something is often as important as what you do.

I have always referred to mediation as "live theater." Most of what happens and is said at mediation is unscripted, unpredictable, and events and words dictate and change what happens next. Mediation is a fluid process. Successful mediators and peacemakers are not "one trick ponies" who utilize a single process to resolve all disputes. Everything is situational and with very little time the mediator must make a series of important process decisions; reacting, of course, to what is unfolding in front of him. Mediators and peacemakers live in the world of "what to do next."

I really began to think about timing as a result of fifty or so co-mediations: Each of us is born with certain instincts and an "internal clock." Some clocks are set faster or slower than others and in our personal lives our internal clocks affect when we do things. But, for purposes of mediation, the point is that everyone has a different clock, including the mediator.

The different clocks became acutely evident to me during my co-mediation experiences. Because mediators have different clocks, co-mediators may have different feelings about "when" to do certain things.

In one co-mediation, I was teamed up with one of the finest mediators in Texas, who was also a very close personal friend and a dear colleague. We "grew up" with mediation together. Although we had been on speaker panels, we had never mediated together. After six rigorous hour of mediation, we found ourselves at a critical point with a CEO of a Fortune 500 company. At that moment, my "clock" told me to move forward and push a little more. Before I could ask my next question, my esteemed and much wiser colleague said, "You know I think we need to take a fifteen minute break." My colleague's "clock" told him this CEO needed space and time for reflection and this is what my co-mediator advised me as we went for a brief walk outside the hotel. My co-mediator believed we needed to be away for thirty minutes because his read was that the CEO was about to make a decision, but needed an opportunity to be alone to get comfortable with his decision. We began talking about timing and other mediation topics. Our conversation was interrupted by the CEO who had come outside to find us. The CEO thanked us for giving him some private time and indicated he was ready to close the deal. Timing was everything in terms of this resolution. Since that moment, I've had the privilege of working with my friend on several occasions. We openly discuss timing and there have been instances where my sense has been right and instances in which my co-mediator's sense has been correct.

The lesson for me in the case I just described is that the mediator, acknowledging that our instincts are essential and often right, still must consciously ask the question "Is this the right time to do this?" Because timing is often critical, I have also frequently suggested that "mediators live in spaces."

What does that mean? Our fantasies of a perfect mediation often envision a seamless process; all the right moves with no disruptions. But, we know that mediation is not seamless, is often unpredictable, and the mediator is reacting instinctively and spontaneously. If timing can either break or make a mediation, the mediator must create space for reflection, the time to at least ask himself "What do I do next?" You ask yourself that question dozens of times during a mediation.

How does a mediator create space? I think there are certain "natural breaks" in every mediation. The first break is immediately after the joint session. The mediator might call a fifteen-minute break for everyone at the close of the joint session. The parties themselves probably need a break, some time to decompress and process what has been said and how they feel. If lawyers are present, the lawyers need some private time to confer with their clients without the mediator present. Equally important, the mediator needs this space to reflect, to plan, and to make process decisions. Every dispute is different and the mediator's approach should be different. During the initial break the mediator is asking, "What do the parties need to happen here?" This question relates specifically to timing. Do the parties need more time together? Do the parties need more time to express their feelings to the mediator in private caucus? Do the parties need more space and a longer break?

Additional "spaces" may occur between caucuses. Mediators need some time after a caucus with a

party to process what has happened and to formulate what to communicate to the other side. These
"spaces" are not thirty-minute breaks, which may
damage momentum. Rather, the mediator might
create a five-minute space for planning and reflection. I have devoted more time to spacing in a later
essay.

Returning to timing, what are some of the timing
issues a mediator might confront?

When to stop a joint session is a timing issue. Has
the content become destructive? Have the parties
stopped listening? Are the parties exhausted, either
physically or emotionally? Has all the information
been exchanged? Or, do the parties simply need a
break and then return to the joint session? The mediator must make these timing decisions.

Part of a mediator's process decisions involves
when to push and when to move back. Mediation is
not always forward motion. In some instances, the
mediator feels the time is right to push the negotiations ahead or more zealously reality test a party.
In other instances, the exact opposite is true; i.e., it
is the wrong time to push and pushing may have a
destructive impact. The parties may need additional
process time before they are ready to close. In this
regard the mediator must critically assess whether
the desire to push is the mediator's clock at work as
opposed to what the parties really need or want to
do. Conversely, the mediator's timing may be off if

the mediator is slowing down the process when the parties are in fact ready to move more quickly.

Timing issues also present themselves in the form of disputants who are operating at very different speeds. The mediator may have a party who wants to take his time and deliberate in one room and a party who wants to cut to the chase in the other room. The more deliberate party will find a more speedy approach intimidating or threatening. The fast paced party may find a slow process frustrating. The mediator must be acutely aware of the party timing differences and confront and acknowledge them. The mediators must focus the parties on the goal of resolution and set a tempo both parties might accept.

Another timing issue is when and if to recess the process when two or three days have been set aside for the mediation. Does the mediator recess at dinnertime or take a supper break and go into the evening? Many mediators believe momentum develops in mediation and a process should continue as long as the parties may tolerate the process. An evening break might damage the momentum, or worse result in backwards movement. But, do the parties need time to reflect before they are ready to the move forward? Does the mediator need some time? Continuing late might, due to fatigue, create an impasse. The timing issue in this regard is purely situational and the mediator must "read" the parties' timing needs.

When to declare recess instead of declaring an impasse is another timing matter. In certain mediations, the parties either are not ready or do not have enough information to resolve the dispute. In such circumstances, pushing towards resolution may create an avoidable impasse. The mediator, as soon as he is aware of such a situation, might advise the parties they need more time to gain information, that a recess is in order, and secure an agreement to return at a specific future date.

Hundreds of other timing issues present themselves to a mediator. Often a mediator, consciously or not, makes dozens of timing decisions during a single mediation. The point remains, however, that when a mediator does something is as important as what the mediator does. The perfect process decision may be ineffective or backfire completely if the timing is not right.

Chapter 5

On Patience

"The waiting is the hardest part"
The Waiting, Tom Petty and the Heartbreakers

Several years ago, a distinguished district judge about to retire made an appointment to see me. The judge, as with many of his collogues, was considering a new career as a mediator.

The judge arrived, punctual as always, with the spiral notebook he often used constantly while on the bench. With his usual solemnity, the judge asked me, "Eric, would you please list in order of priority, the essential characteristics of a mediator."

Thankfully, I had a quick answer for His Honor. I had published a short list of ten essential mediator qualities years ago.

"I always begin, Your Honor, with patience. A mediator must always be patient," I responded.

The judge closed his notebook immediately.

"We do not need to go any farther. Perhaps I

should pursue my semi-retirement as an arbitrator," the judge said.

And, with that, the judge stood up, shook my hand and left. I see this judge each year at an annual Christmas party. The judge gladly tells this story to anyone who will listen. The judge has become a very skilled arbitrator; but, he does not mediate.

So much of mediation training and mediation writing deals with what a mediator should do and the phases of the mediation process. Precious little has been written about the essential quality of patience. Patience is a rare quality in society today. We have become accustomed, largely due to technology, to instantaneous communication of information. We also have been accustomed to obtaining information in sound bytes. We are a "just get to it" society, often in a hurry.

Problem-solving and dispute resolution involve an opposite discipline. Dispute resolution takes time. One may not rush effective problem solving. And, as a result, dispute resolution requires patience.

Who must be patient? Certainly, the mediator must be patient. The disputants must be patient. And, the disputants' legal representatives, their lawyers, must be patient.

As you must intuitively understand, patience has become an unnatural state of being for most mere mortals. Who among you as not heard, two or three hours into a mediation, "We are just wasting our time"? The inherent conflict between an impatient society and a process that demands patience creates a tension that the mediator must deal with.

As with everything, the initial inquiry regarding patience must begin with the process caretaker, the mediator. Mediators must acknowledge, because they are part of society that they themselves may be as impatient as the disputants who appear before them. A mediator may delude himself to believe that while he may be impatient in his personal affairs that he is entirely patient in his professional role. At best, such a proclamation is a rationalization. At worst, a mediator is confessing an almost schizophrenic state in which she does not "walk her own talk." Patience is a discipline practiced both on the clock and off the clock. If a mediator loses his temper because a bank teller takes too long to process a transaction, the mediator may lose his temper during a frustrating moment at mediation.

So why do we become impatient? What does that mean exactly?

I think that patience defined both broadly and non-scientifically, means things aren't going as fast as we would like them to go. Someone does not understand us quickly enough. Someone is not "getting it." Someone is not doing what we think they should do as quickly as we think they should. Our own needs are creating a temporal agenda in which we hope, if not expect, that others should conform.

But, an appreciation of diversity teaches us to dismiss such expectations. Everyone operates and functions at their own speed. Everyone processes and deals with every human activity at their own rate of speed. And, some people feel badly that we live in a "cut to the chase" society and no one gets to tell their story at the tempo he wants to tell it. We will discuss listening later; but part of listening is the feeling that no one takes the time.

I know better than to ask whether you have taken the time to hear your spouse, your child, your significant other, your business partner, or anyone else. We are so busy. We do not have enough time. Time is precious. How much time would it take you to express how you feel about the loss of a child or a failed business transaction that decimated your family? How would you feel if someone invited you to share such things in under ten minutes?

And, are you able to tell when someone is becoming impatient with you? Do you notice the body language? Does the indifference hurt? How does that make you feel? We mediators say the pledge of allegiance to neutrality and confidentiality? Is patience less important?

What are the implications of impatience? If the patience problem is that things aren't going quickly enough for the mediator, the patience problem is owned by the mediator. Mediation has nothing to do with what the mediator wants or needs.

The discipline of patience for mediation begins with this essential proposition. Every disputant is entitled to take whatever time he feels is necessary to tell his story and to analyze and solve his problem. The mediator must make himself available unconditionally to the disputant in this regard.

Why is this so important? If the mediator imposes her own temporal agenda, she is consciously or unconsciously, becoming judgmental. People who are hurried or rushed perceive, rightfully or wrongfully, that what they are saying or doing is unimportant or wrong. People, in such instances, feel judged, cut off, and abandoned. What this is not about is the mediator's clock. What this is entirely about is the disputant's clock.

I am a strong believer that the mediator may offer the least expensive gifts that many humans crave. The first of the gifts is patience. People just expect the opposite. The initial evidence of lack of caring, at least to them, is impatience. Patience in mediation is a wonderful oasis in a compressed, hurried world. This is one of the least explored reasons that mediation is a different paradigm. Mediation allows the time that virtually nothing else does.

A mediator must therefore embrace patience as one of the most powerful and singularly important attributes of the process. Mediators must practice and preach patience because of its uniqueness and because it is a powerful aide in resolving disputes.

But what about the patience of the parties, or for that matter, the parties' lawyers? You may be thinking that while the mediator must practice patience, don't the parties suffer from the same problem? The simple answer is "yes."

The other facet of patience is that many people demand patience from others but do not give it back in return. Most people impose their own sense of timing on others. For the mediator who practices patience, this reality imposes certain challenges.

The disputants themselves may have different "clocks." Certain disputants approach problem solving quickly. Such disputants want to just "get down to it." Other disputants approach problem solving more slowly and methodically. During a mediation a mediator may encounter a room in which things aren't going fast enough and a room in which things are moving to quickly. And lawyers, and this is an admitted generalization, are frequently impatient.

The solution to this problem, and this will be a theme throughout these essays, is that a mediator must be a teacher of disciplines; in this instance, patience. And, the mediator has an array of methods to accomplish this mission. Everything in life is inevitably a "compared to what." In the context of a dispute, the patience question is what happens next if we do not take the time to resolve this matter? Far more often than not, the time taken at mediation is a microchip of time compared to what happens next.

Hours at mediation compare favorably to months and probably years of litigation. Mediators may offer this perspective which inspires patience.

Mediators teach patience by demonstrating patience. Parties become frustrated during mediation and often look to see whether the mediator is frustrated. At such moments, the mediator should acknowledge the parties frustrations but encourage the parties to understand that the mediator must remain patient with the process and that difficult problems require time to solve. The mediator might remind the parties that patience is often rewarded and the time savings that resolution will afford to all.

One must also consider that a complex dispute may not be resolvable in an eight or ten-hour day. Often, the dispute has been brewing for years, with litigation extending the life of the dispute. An attempt to create a resolution in eight hours may be the very thing that creates an artificial impasse. The mediator needs to be the arbiter of just how much time the process will take and urge the parties to remain patient.

Inevitably, the disputants come to admire the patience of a mediator and begin to demonstrate patience. Because patience is such a rare quality, disputants become more committed to a process that offers something special. Many disputants, at the close of a mediation, will actually acknowledge the mediator's patience, perhaps leaving the process a bit more patient themselves.

A mediator, in this regard, is like an experienced fisherman. A fisherman may have to throw his line in the water dozens of times, waiting hours to get a bite. The fisherman and the mediator, beyond anything else, must be patient.

Chapter 6

On People Moving

"Someone's waiting just for you
spinning wheel, spinning true."
Spinning Wheel, Blood Sweat & Tears

Mediation is not a static process. Mediation is a fluid process. Why then should parties remain in one place for the majority of the process? Why shouldn't environments change? Why shouldn't the configurations of the parties change? Mediators, whether they know it or not, are in the people moving business. "People moving" does not only mean motivating, assisting, and empathizing. "People moving" may also mean physically changing combinations of people in order to find the right "matches" or moving people into a different environment to change the mood or the feel of the conversation. "People moving" as you will see, might include having the parties dine together or it might include a long walk outside. The theory is that one way to change a static conversation or dig the parties out of a rut is to change the scenery or the people combinations.

I have devoted an entire essay on environment; but, let's give environment a different spin in terms of people moving during the process.

Suppose you have planned a trip to New York City to do some sightseeing. The day you arrive the weather changes and it begins to rain torrentially. You stare out of your room window. The weather is so bad you cannot go out. After two or three hours, your room seems to be much smaller. You finally go down to the lobby and you suddenly feel a little better. Other people are around. The scenery is different. It's still raining cats and dogs but somehow the relocation to the lobby makes it all manageable.

To some extent, disputants on their first trip to Mediationland may feel the same way. Most mediators have no idea how a disputant feels during a mediation, unless a mediator has actually been a party to a mediation. I have, in a small commercial dispute. My mediation took place after I had mediated over 500 cases. Our mediator was an excellent mediator who I know and respect deeply. But, the mediation felt very different as a party.

First, the mediation process seems to go in slow motion, especially when the mediator is not in your room. We were placed in a nice enough room. But, the room seemed to grow smaller and there didn't seem to be any place to go. Once split into separate rooms, we stayed in that room for nine hours. I have never been to jail; but, that's what it almost felt like. I had a desire at some point to see some of the people in the other room. I never saw them once after the joint session. Apparently, after 6:00pm the other group ordered out for Chinese. We saw the delivery-man go down the hall. The food smelled great. We moved rapidly from jealousy to anger. The longer we remained in the same room, the more our words and conversations remained the same. Guest appearances from the mediator became monotonous. We never reached the point where we agreed to settle just to be released. And, the case settled. The settlement was very fair. We mostly were focusing on the Chinese food we didn't get. We all were very glad to make our escape.

As a mediator, I thought of the irony of it all a week later. First, the dispute was an extremely difficult one to settle. The mediator must have been dog-tired and had kept going until it resolved. I suspect the mediator left that evening believing that everyone thought he did a great job. But all we ever talked about after the fact was what a miserable day and evening it was.

Admittedly, Mediationland is not Disneyland; but, are we aware of how dreadful the experience may feel to the parties?

People moving, in the environmental sense, is intended to defeat the agony of semi-imprisonment;

but, more important, like set change in the theater an environmental change impacts mood, conversation, and attitudes.

So what might a mediator do in this regard? Of course, parties also get attached to and feel safer in their "home bases." But, nothing prevents you, for a variety of reasons, from changing things around. Think outside the box.

We have a wonderful coffee shop across the deck from our mediation center. Sometimes, I take a party across the deck and talk in the coffee shop. If I do it with one party, I do it with the other party. Everything just feels different. The tone of the conversation changes. A little chocolate cheesecake elevates the spirits and the blood sugar levels.

Sometimes, a good walk with a party makes all the difference. The physical aspects of walking gets the blood flowing. Tone always changes when you change from conversation in a room to chatting as you are walking. And, a good walk may also have additional benefits.

Let's move from the environmental aspect of people moving and to changing combinations of parties. Permit me to start with an illustration that leads to the benefits of a good walk.

You are mediating a dispute in which a school board is the plaintiff. The chairperson of the school board (in this instance male), several board members, and two outside counsel, are present at the mediation. After an extensive initial private caucus, you determine several things. First the chairman of the school board is the sole decision-maker. Second, everyone else in his group is terrified of the chairperson and will agree with whatever he says. Third, the chairperson is emboldened by his fawning group and enjoys showing them how tough he is. Fourth, the chairperson is a personality you've seen before; i.e., tough guy, controlling, needs to feel important, but also secretly appreciates no nonsense people who are willing to look him in the eye and speak very candidly.

You may not, of course, shame the chairman in front of his group. But, you may identify him as terribly important, invite him for a private meeting (his group will be appreciative), and go for a walk.

What are you doing? You are removing the chairman from an audience he will play to all day long. You are identifying his importance. You are taking the chairperson away from a physical room he controls. And, you are providing yourself an opportunity to be who the chairman needs you to be without risking any embarrassment,

So what happens next? You walk a bit. You stop. You look the chairman in the eye and say " You know, I'm thinking you are tired of listening to all this nonsense. Don't you think it's time to cut through the B.S. and figure a way to settle this mess? I'm sure you're sick of paying lawyers and this has got to be a drain on your valuable time."

You will notice, far more likely than not, the chairman's body language will change and equally likely he will agree he wants this mess over with. You will let the chairman know you really want to help him achieve that goal and you might ask "What do you really need to come out of this in one piece?" My prediction is that the rhetoric and posturing will stop, largely due to the creation of a new dynamic that the chairman will appreciate and understand. Essentially, you have created a different world, a world in which something may be done.

Mediators, I believe, should be constantly searching for winning combinations of people in order to create the right dynamic for resolution. Let me offer you a few illustrations of people moving which created the dynamic necessary for resolution.

Consider a very large construction dispute in which the parties and their counsel brought their expert (and expert witnesses) engineers to the mediation. The dispute involved the alleged failure of a heating and cooling system for a complex of very large buildings. As you are aware lawyers frequently criticize the other side's experts and experts rarely get to visit with each other. But, generally speaking, who are engineers? Engineers are problem solvers who either design or fix things. In this instance the complex owner really wanted the system fixed; but, the entire focus of the litigation had been on assessing blame and alleging faulty system design instead of repair. During the joint session at which the engineer spoke, the engineers all hinted that the system could in fact be fixed. With the permission of the parties and as part of the mediation process, I dispatched the experts into a separate room and gave them a group assignment; namely, what would be the best way to fix the system. Meanwhile I continued the process with the lawyers and parties.

I noticed when the engineers were placed in their room they seemed genuinely excited and expressly appreciative of being assigned the roles of problem solvers instead of as hired guns. My faith in the engineers was not misplaced. Less than three hours later, the engineers asked to meet with the entire group. Rather proudly, the engineers had developed a consensus solution to repair the system and had even created a timetable and estimated budget for repair.

With the help of the engineers, the mediation process went smoothly and effortlessly through the remaining issues and two hours later the parties completely resolved their dispute. The trick was simply people moving and finding the right combination for the particular dispute. The engineers arrived at a creative solution that parties locked in their rooms engaged in traditional distributive negotiation would never have found.

Another illustration of the benefit of an effective combination was a class action Americans with Disabilities claim against a major university. The court required all officers of the university, including its President, to be present for five full days of mediation. The court further required all necessary students to attend the mediation with full decision-making authority. During the first private caucus with the university officials it became apparent that several thought the discussions about toilet stalls to be trivial. I asked the University President whether he preferred to shut the door when he went to the restroom. The President laughed and said "Of course."

I next visited with the student group and asked whether they would assist with a small experiment. I asked one student whether he would let the President borrow his motorized wheel chair and try to navigate it into a restroom stall and close the door. The student, an engineering major, readily agreed.

I brought all parties together and told them what were about to do. The University President agreed. The President, with about sixty of us in his wake, motored to the men's restroom down the hall and, after some difficulty, entered the restroom. Even with navigational and friendly advice from students, the President finally managed to barely squeeze into the stall after ten minutes. And, of course, the restroom door could not even come close to being shut. At the moment of defeat, the President looked up, smiled, and said "We need to fix this. We need to make it all right." The light went on. To his great credit, the President, with students as helpers and friends, became a student and voracious learner himself. Doorknobs suddenly became important when he could not open the door to a classroom with a closed fist. On a deeper level, the President began to feel both the student's frustrations and isolation. Whenever during the process we got stuck, the President asked if he could meet with "his students." The combination simply worked and as an element of the final settlement the parties agreed to a dispute resolution process.

In another instance, both inside counsel and all principle decision makers were women. The legion of all outside counsel was men. The dispute involved a situation in which the parties would have an ongoing, long-term business relationship regardless of the outcome at trial.

The joint session produced several revelations. The women did not like the approach of the male lawyers, their own included. The male lawyers did not understand at all what was important to their female counterparts nor had they even bothered to ask. The male lawyers had no idea how their female counterparts wanted to negotiate or problem solve. The joint session lasted nearly three hours and brought us right up to lunch.

One of the male lawyers looked up at me and asked, "So what do we do next?" I pointed to the six women and said, "The six of you go to lunch, outside this building. Return whenever you wish." The male lawyers looked puzzled and concerned, but the women were all smiles and already halfway out the door. That moment produced a classic mediation line. One woman looked at me and asked, "May we also go shop for shoes after lunch?" I was advised later more specifically of the significance of that question. The combination, not surprisingly, worked. The women returned four hours later, announced the agreement they had reached, and instructed the male lawyers to draft an agreement and not "screw things up." Forgive me. I do not know whether any shoes were purchased.

One postscript on the shoe saga, I sometimes, in appropriate cases, have the parties eat lunch together. The simple human act of having a meal together breaks barriers, allows parties to see each other differently, and often results in conversation which greatly assists the chances of resolutions. Meals allow people to discuss their children, where they're from, their interests and passions. Often the sharing of this information creates a connection and may provide the mediator with combination alternatives.

Finally, lawyers sometimes need to be combined for a meeting when it is apparent that there is something wrong between them. As a former litigator, I understand how things can go wrong between lawyers, even lawyers who are highly professional, ethical, and maybe even very good friends.

I recall one late evening when two of the finest lawyers I know, and who were very close friends, nearly got into a fistfight. The two lawyers' children were friends and the lawyers often went to football games together. But, the lawyers had been in the case for three years, both with very difficult clients. We were inches away from finalizing a deal which both lawyers had helped in a valiant way to put together. But, something strange happened. One of the lawyers, a business lawyer, and a legendary scrivener, was marking up settlement language prepared by his dear friend and making copious grammatical corrections. The other lawyer finally couldn't stand it any longer and stormed into his friend's room. Fortunately, I was in that room. The lawyer's words were harsh, personal and loud, the opposite of this lawyer's very being. His friend shot up from his seat and shouted back. The moment resembled a gunfight in a Texas saloon. I grabbed both lawyers, literally, and I took them into the kitchen. I handed each a beer and we adjourned to my office. The next thirty minutes involved a lot of apologies, reminiscing about how they both usually drove each other crazy, and a bunch of talk about how much they respected each other. We co-drafted the final two provisions over the second beer. I do not insinuate alcohol in my mediations. This was my first and only time. But, it was very late, we had only two more provisions to draft, and the combination of good friends and a cold one, as we refer to it Texas, just seemed right.

So, if you are at home, twist open a longneck. Here's to people moving!

Chapter 7

On Spaces

"What shall we use to fill the empty spaces
where we used to talk?"
Empty Spaces, Pink Floyd

Mediators are so much in the spotlight during a mediation that mediators need to create spaces for reflection. Certainly, a mediator may not disappear for prolonged periods of time; but, a mediator needs to create space both for himself and the parties during the process. The parties also have a need on their own to process information and reflect.

The mediator may create a very necessary opportunity for reflection after an extended joint session. Joint sessions provide the parties with a tremendous amount of information to process and consider. Some joint sessions may be extremely emotional and the parties need a chance to calm down. Also, if the parties are represented by counsel, disputants will want private time with their counsel. Of course, the disputants may need some time to meet certain human needs after the joint sessions; i.e. get some coffee, restroom, smoke, get some fresh air, etc.

Similarly, the mediator needs space to process what she has just heard and to formulate a game plan. Fifteen minutes seems to be a perfect amount of time for this.

For a mediator, the post joint session space allows for several important things to take place.

A mediator usually has no idea what a dispute is really about, or what is driving the dispute, until he meets the disputants and observes and listens to them during the joint session. In fact, a mediator should approach a mediation, regardless of what she has read, with this very state of mind. The joint session provides the mediator with the first glimpse of the dynamics. What did the parties and their lawyers say? What did they really mean? What did the participants' body language tell you? How did the participants interact? What are the critical factual and legal issues? How is the mediator going to fashion a relationship with both sides? Are there important non-monetary interests? What have the economic negotiations been? What is the appropriate initial approach? Has the story been told completely? How are the participants adjusting to the process? Who will make the decisions?

The above questions are only a partial list; but, the mediator needs time to arrive at a tentative initial plan. Really, when one thinks that a lawyer has months or years in a particular dispute to anticipate and plan, one must conclude that it is quite amazing that an experienced mediator may assimilate so much so quickly and usually react correctly.

Another logical space is after your first caucus with a party but before an offer is made. Caucuses often result in re-evaluation and reconsideration. What a party thought they might demand or offer may change. The party needs space to consider this and the mediator buys some time. Spacing allows the parties necessary time for reflection.

In many instances, parties desire feedback from the mediator as to whether an offer or counter-offer will be helpful. The mediator's first private caucus with each party is usually a very significant event in the process. The initial caucus is usually when trust building begins in earnest. The first caucus is also the moment when a mediator begins to truly know how the parties really feel. The first caucus marks the beginning of reality testing and re-evaluation. Assuming reality testing has resulted in re-evaluation, it is unrealistic to assume the parties will be willing to share these new feelings with the mediator and the parties may need time to reach new conclusions.

Capable mediators know when to excuse themselves from a room. A mediator might say "You know we've covered a lot of territory. Let me give you some time to consider what we've discussed and I'll return to discuss what sort of proposal you want to make." As discussed in another essay, a great deal of action takes place when a mediator is not in the room. Spacing allows for this part of the process to occur.

Similar spaces are necessary throughout the caucus process. For example, a mediator submits a new proposal. A mediator should remain in the room to observe the initial reaction. But, the mediator should make an exit to allow the parties an opportunity to discuss and digest the proposal. The mediator also wants to avoid receiving a knee jerk reaction to a proposal.

Probably the most difficult spacing issue, and it is also a timing matter, is whether to continue a mediation (usually into the late evening or early morning) or declare a recess with a specific commitment by the parties to return another day.

Most mediators believe, correctly so, that momentum builds during the mediation process and that serious negotiations do not begin until late in the day. During a mediation, many barriers to resolution are broken, re-evaluation occurs, and the parties become increasingly committed to the process. Many mediators believe that declaring a recess destroys momentum and creates the danger that the parties will return to the positions they held before the mediation. I think most of the time plunging forward is the best course; but, as with all things in mediation such a determination is purely situational.

In <u>certain</u> cases, the decision to press forward may actually create an impasse. The parties may simply be too tired to make the remaining decisions. Or the mediation has created a great deal of progress and bridged huge gaps; but, the parties honestly need some time to reflect. In such cases, a recess which allows for some re-evaluation is always better than driving the parties to impasse. And, when you think about it, why should a dispute which had existed for years necessarily be resolved in eight to fifteen hours? Many disputes may be resolved within such time parameters. But, certain disputes need space to breathe.

One technique to avoid confusion or backsliding after a recess is for the mediator to draft a memorandum at the close of the session. Such memorandum memorializes the negotiation positions of the parties when they adjourned, a commitment to leave those positions on the table for a stated time (the close of the second mediation or if the mediator declares an impasse), identification of any information which should be exchanged or discovery which should occur prior to the second session, and an agreement to resume the mediation on a particular date.

Creating "spaces" is helpful both to the mediator and the parties and should be integrated into your process.

Chapter 8

On Environment

"Changes in latitudes"
Changes in Latitudes, Changes in Attitudes,
Jimmy Buffett

Communication between the mediator and the parties occurs on many levels. What does the mediator's environment, the place the mediator does his work, communicate to the parties?

We know, of course, how environments impact us. We know how our favorite French or Italian restaurant makes us feel. We know how walking into a courtroom impacts people. You know the feeling you get when you walk into a "friendly" pediatrician's office. What exactly does a mediator wish his environment to communicate? What effect does the mediator wish for his environment to have on the people who enter it? And, if you mediate court-annexed cases, who are you trying to impact? The lawyers? The parties? Or both?

The initial analysis should focus on the parties.

The parties come from all walks of life. Likely, the people who enter your facility are a microcosm of society. If this diverse group has anything in common, they are likely apprehensive, nervous, and probably have no frame of reference of what a mediation center even looks like. Some people may think, rather erroneously, that a mediation center might look like a law office or even a courtroom.

I think the mediation environment should have two primary goals; i.e. to relax and calm the parties and to humanize and make the mediator accessible. Every environment tells a story and you need to decide what story your environment will tell. I think, especially for mediators who are lawyers or former judges, that there is an initial inclination towards a highly professional office, something lawyers and their large institutional clients will find familiar and comfortable. Such an environment conveys the message "I'm successful, I'm important, and I'm a professional just like you." But, such an environment may be intimidating to some or even imply a bias of some sort. More important, such an environment may not calm or humanize.

I will overcome my initial reluctance to say this so plainly; but, it's what I really believe. Mediation is a different paradigm. Shouldn't the mediation environment necessarily be a different and suggest a different paradigm? Shouldn't the mediation environment suggest something different is in play the moment parties step foot inside your office? I am not suggesting the bizarre or strange; but, I am advocating lateral thinking and creativity. Because the parties have no frame of reference for a mediation center and you are attempting to communicate a message, you may dare to be different. Creativity and professionalism are not mutually exclusive. And, from a marketing perspective, a different, effective mediation environment may be one way to distinguish your practice. Favorable environments are memorable and make people wish to return. A lawyer might think, "My clients really like Jeff's office, so I need to keep taking them there."

In terms of environment, you have dozens of choices to make; but, these choices may be divided into the following groups; rooms, common spaces, colors, furnishings, fabrics, decorations, and "just things."

Let's begin with "just things", because they are the most fun and the easiest things to add if you are not designing an environment from square one. And, as I hope you will see, little changes may have a great impact.

What exactly are "just things"? Just things is the stuff you place around your mediation office that tells people something about the process, something about you, or something that will either amuse, entertain, or educate them. I know what some of you are initially thinking; i.e., diplomas, plaques, certificates attesting to your unparalleled accomplishments. These things might go somewhere less conspicuous; but, we're trying to build bridges and not create barriers.

Photographs are really good things, because as Rod Stewart said, "every picture tells a story, don't it?" People just like looking at pictures and pictures allow people access. Pictures of children, grandchildren, nephews, and nieces are terrific. Most people love children, and love looking at photographs of children. Children's photographs make people feel happy, more cheerful, and more relaxed. Most people have children, grandchildren, nephews, and nieces. People, I believe, trust people who are proud of and display their children. Photographs of children almost invite a response. Many people will want to show you pictures of their children and, when they do, a conversation usually ensues.

What about photographs of the mediator? Photographs that tell a story and build bridges instead of barriers may have a favorable impact. If you run marathons, a photo of you crossing the finish line tells an interesting story. If you coach a youth soccer team, a photo of you with your team grants access. If you love to travel, a photograph of you in front of the Eiffel Tower opens a door to conversation. You get the idea. And, lest I be accused of being forgetful, a photo of your spouse or significant other is warm and invites conversation. Most people are visual and these are visual cues which create feelings, open up doors to who you are, create impressions, and allow for conversation when things get stuck.

But, be even more daring and creative. What things do you really love when you are not working? What are the things you care about, serious or otherwise?

I love music. I am especially addicted to Bruce Springsteen. I think music connects people. I am fascinated that thousands of people will hear the same song and love it for entirely different reasons. Music evokes memories, feelings, and perspectives. Many people remember exactly where they were the first time they heard a Beatles song. Music relaxes people. Music cheers people up. Music may help people through tough times.

So we have music symbols throughout our mediation center. Of course, we have the "Springsteen Shrine", an autographed picture of the E-Street Band surrounded by the Boss's CD's. We have the Bob Marley, Jimmy Buffet, and Led Zeppelin sections. And, we felt the moral obligation after their recent flap to have a Dixie Chicks autographed photo. We have a Beatles Wall. We now have drumsticks and other musical objects. The responses to our "music things" are varied and always positive. A stoic, well-dressed banker told me where he was when he saw Led Zeppelin for the first time. I learned that the stoic banker was very different than the man wearing a very expensive suit. The banker learned how much I enjoy music. We both disclosed we looked very different thirty years ago. We had not spoken a substantive word about the dispute; but, we had rapidly created a bond and a communication. As it turned out, discussing the dispute became easy; but, we were annoyed that our continuing music discussion had to be interrupted.

Things might also include artifacts or objects you picked up on a trip, things you have made, or other tangible symbols of your passions, subject to obvious rules of political correctness. But, "things," as I've described them, create conversation, help establish trust, and make you less of a stranger.

Some mediators favor things parties can do, so they are not bored or so that they may become more relaxed. Games, toys, books, videos are all things that some mediators have in their offices.

Other mediators have things that people may eat, understanding that people do eat when they are nervous and eating keeps energy levels up. A great mediator in Dallas loaned me his very professional office to conduct a mediation. He had canisters of hard to find candy and snacks everywhere. The parties ogled over this confectionary feast and partook frequently. My impression was that this favorably impacted their attitudes. I don't believe sugar highs, mine included, adversely affected problem solving.

Let's move to decorations, fabrics, and furnishings. I must confess neither I nor my colleagues are decorators; but, I can tell you what we were aiming for- warmth. We wanted warm colors, warm textures, warm fabrics, and warm furnishings. We wanted the overall tone to make people walk in and instantly be comfortable. We were hoping to make people feel more like they were at home than at an office. We think we've succeeded in favorably impacting moods and attitudes when people walk in. People find the atmosphere to be inviting, not intimidating.

As for rooms, a mixture of different types of rooms may create different atmospheres. In our center, we do have traditional large conference rooms for joint sessions involving multiple parties and complex cases. But, the breakout rooms, while nicely furnished, more resemble dens, with sofas and plush chairs which allow disputants to feel more relaxed. The external environment, what is outside your office, is often dictated by circumstance and what is available. When we decided to start a purely mediation firm, we searched long and hard for something other than the twenty-second floor of an office building downtown. All of us had mediated in such places and felt that parties begin to feel claustrophobic and shut in as the day progressed. We wanted an open environment and through sheer accident found one.

Our mediation center is in a quaint complex with

a coffee shop and two restaurants abutting Lake Austin. Our conference rooms overlook the river and the boat docks and the views are fantastic. More important, water is calming and parties may walk out onto a sprawling deck and sit on picnic tables by the water. I can't tell you how many settlements have been achieved at 4:00 pm on a picnic table by the river; but, we believe the environmental factor plays some part in the process. We are often asked if we have a boat. The answer, as of this writing, is "no"; but, we plan to have one and incorporate it into the process. We named our office The Lakeside Mediation Center and it has developed an identity. I write about Lakeside purely as an illustration of creativity and the part environment may and does play in the mediation process. We also enjoy the fact that we are in a public setting and literally tens of thousands of people get to see the word <u>mediation</u> each year. We do not take walk-in business. Many people who do walk in out of curiosity believe, despite the prominent sign, that it is a meditation center. We do like the feeling that mediation, because of where we are located, is part "of the people." If you would like to see what the Lakeside environment actually looks like, you may take a tour on our website at <u>www. gcbmediators.com</u>

The mediation environment will not, in and of itself, be determinative of outcomes. But the mediation environment does impact the process, the parties, and also very favorably affects the mediators.

Chapter 9

On Apology and Forgiveness

"It's times like these you learn to live again."
Times Like These, Foo Fighters

As I was writing this book, I was asked to be a panelist on the topic of apology and forgiveness for a mediation conference in New York City. I wrote a short story based on a real case for that presentation and it follows these first few paragraphs. The story demonstrates the power of people under extraordinary circumstances to make an apology and to offer forgiveness. The real mediation stayed with me for a very long time and I was glad to have an excuse to write the story.

Initially, I was intending to make the story this essay because I think the bravery of the women best captures anything I could possibly say. And, I have not spent years researching the philosophical, religious, and spiritual nature of apology and forgiveness. I've just observed hundreds of people who behave more courageously than I think I ever could.

Their courage has made me more optimistic about the human condition and more hopeful.

I believe that one of the unique ways that human beings demonstrate grace and their most spiritual selves is by making a sincere apology and by granting forgiveness. These acts seem to acknowledge what we all know to be true; i.e. we are imperfect, we make mistakes, sometimes terrible harm is caused, and we have the true capacity to forgive. The process of apology and forgiveness is extraordinarily powerful and sometimes difficult to even imagine.

I recall a case of a world class ob-gyn who had successfully delivered a couple's first three children. This doctor epitomized everything good about physicians. Brilliant, skilled, thorough, warm, caring and kind. This physician enjoyed a wonderful relationship with this family. But, this doctor, as are we all, was also human. On this particular day and after thousands of successful deliveries, this doctor's humanity caught up with him. On this tragic day, the doctor made a serious mistake and this couple's fourth child, a son, died thirty minutes after delivery.

The doctor was discouraged by a hospital administrator from expressing his regret and grief to the family he cared for so deeply after the child passed away. The couple felt brushed off, ignored, and seemingly betrayed by a dear friend. Because of this, the couple, devout Catholics, retained a lawyer to file a malpractice claim.

During the years of discovery and depositions, the doctor was torn up over his inability to go to the family and confess his mistake, express his grief over the tragedy, acknowledge their loss, and seek forgiveness. The family also suffered. The family, of course, was grieving the loss of their beloved child. But, the family was also agonizing over something else. The family, because of their faith, had an unconditional obligation to forgive their friend. How could they do so if he never came to them and made such a request?

The initial phases of this mediation did not allow for this opportunity. The lawyers, as they sometimes do, specifically discouraged the parties from speaking at the joint session. While I do not condone such discouragement, I understand it. Lawyers believe their responsibility is to protect their clients. Despite the confidentiality of mediation, lawyers worry that disclosures by clients may make them more exposed. And, with no interaction between the parties and because liability was virtually conceded for purposes of mediation, the dispute was resolved for the payment of a certain sum in less than five hours.

As the lawyers were crafting a mediation agreement, I was in the doctor's room and once again witnessed the majesty and power of human beings.

I could tell the doctor was unhappy and asked him why. He responded, "The settlement doesn't end this for me. I had hoped for more out of this today. I really need to talk with the family." After his lawyers advised the doctor that the settlement was complete and such a meeting was not necessary, the doctor insisted I ask the family if they would be willing to meet.

The family as it turned out, had had similar discussions with their lawyer. As I walked in, the mother looked at me and said "I want to meet with my doctor."

A meeting was arranged without the lawyers. I remained in the room to see what happened. The doctor broke down in tears and began sobbing that he was sorry, so very sorry. The mother got up and opened her arms. The doctor went to her and they embraced. The mother, then the father, told the doctor "We forgive you." It seemed as if during these powerful moments that the family felt the profound need to console their doctor and help him through this. As the family was doing this, the family was also finding closure. But, it was also something else. This moment was an act of grace, something that human beings have a need and an ability to do if only they are afforded the opportunity.

As our world seems to be spinning out of control with seemingly escalating and endless violence and conflict, I hold on to such moments because they inspire me to believe in our potential, our possibilities, and our indelible ability to express our grace, our kindness, and compassion. I would like to believe that as stewards of the mediation process we can play some part in this evolution, this expectancy. We should not coerce or compel people who have no interest in such an exchange to do so. But, when people hope that the process will allow for such expression, we are failing participants if we do not provide a forum and opportunity for this to occur.

The story which follows is another illustration of this power and grace. Sometimes we have a larger obligation than simply settling a lawsuit. Something more important needs to take place. We need to be ready and available for such moments.

Chapter 10

A Meeting of Strangers

Christmas was coming to West Texas just like it always did. The harsh, cold winds from the west had already cloaked the unforgiving landscape with an extra layer of dust that Virginia Stevens had to sweep off her front porch at least three times a day. As if Ginny didn't already have more than enough to do this time of year.

Nothing much had changed in Odessa, Ginny thought, as she glanced at the same suspended holiday lights that she remembered from high school and maybe even from before that. What was that anyway? Thirty? Forty years? No point in trying to recall exactly. As her doctor husband Bill would say, "Just a damn long time ago." The old nativity scene sure could use a new coat of paint, Ginny also thought as her Saturn breezed by the Catholic Church. And that manger sure looked droopy and nothing like the heavenly home she conjured up in October when she felt Christmas coming hard like a train rolling fast down the track.

Well, West Texas was still pretty much the same. Sure, the inevitable and sometimes convenient Wal-Mart's, Applebee's, and even a Target Superstore now dotted the landscape. But, the landscape remained sorry, flat, and yes, hopelessly dusty. The dust was such a problem for those baby doctors' wives from Dallas who Ginny, along with the West Texas Medical Recruiting Committee, tried to convince to settle and raise their families in Odessa instead of those green lawns in Highland Park that seemed to hiss in the summers. For heavens sake, the town fathers had even built a special subdivision to recruit doctors, with man-made lakes and artificial "rolling hills." Actually, they looked more like uneven mounds of dirt; but, they called it "Pill Hill" and at least a few of the Dallas wives seemed to like it.

But, most folks who loved this place were born here, grew up here, raised their kids, and were buried a few miles from the house they grew up in. Sometimes it felt like one of those dumb movies in which someone goes back into the past, but the past is the present, and it all ends up in one big stinking mess that was way too confusing to try to figure out.

When out of town folks conjured up stereotypes of Texas and came to Odessa, visitors were rarely disappointed. West Texas was a large place with an open sky and where big men still walked the land, trying often to lasso oil from terrible holes in desolate country. Ten minutes outside Odessa you could set the car cruise control on 85 and drive for over an hour and not see much of anything. Friday nights were only about high school football. And, yes, when folks got divorced, and yes that happened way too much in Ginny's humble opinion, they'd go to court and fight over the football tickets. To heck with the kids and where they'd live. Ginny's brother John had disgraced the family and become a lawyer. John had spent two full weeks in court in Midland trying to convince twelve good citizens that old man Williams was not in his right mind when he bequeathed the season tickets to his daughter Susie instead of his son Alex.

And John, like all West Texas men, especially the lawyers, could sure tell a story. Ginny no longer could excuse them by describing the stories as tall tales. Ginny now called John's stories whoppers, which grew as large as a triple meat, double cheese Number Three at the Burger King by the time John got finished. John, who had passed not so gently through sixty, was obsessed with the "old days when lawyers were really lawyers." Ginny thought she'd just have a stroke if she heard another story about drinking all night on the long train ride to El Paso and trying your case badly hung over. "And as the fog would lift around eleven," John would say, "I knew I was going to win that damn case."

The worst part was that John somehow managed to win most of his cases stinking drunk but that did not prevent Ginny from reminding her brother that in most ways he was as sorry as it gets.

Saturdays were mostly spent at the Odessa Country Club. The men would golf, usually badly but lie about it, and the women would start with tea and charity talk and migrate to gin and tonic and pondering who was having an affair with whom and blame it all on whiskey, the modern destruction of proper society, and three well known bars three miles outside of town.

Sunday was church. Visitors never had to trouble themselves about finding religion here. By last count, 87 churches existed to support the need of 57,523 citizens who had a whole lot of confessing to do and required an awful lot of forgiveness.

Ginny also couldn't figure out why, at sixty-five years of age and, albeit the matriarch of a very large family, she was still responsible for Christmas dinner. Adding up the grandkids, her allegedly grown kids and their spouses and even ex-spouses, and purported family who claimed an invitation by about ten degrees of separation, Ginny was going to feed something near ninety bodies, all of whom came as if they had eaten their last meal on Thanksgiving – which also, by the way, was at her house. But, West Texans don't complain out loud much. They moan a lot to the Lord and maybe whimper a bit to their very best friend. And even in moments of terrible crisis, West Texans never wear their hearts on their sleeves. Life is tough. Life ain't fair. And, you just put on your boots, roll up your sleeves, and do what you have to do.

Just when Ginny was beginning to feel that mythical sense of resolve and developing the usual delusion that she would once again pull off Christmas dinner, she remembered the three bean casserole and the absolutely, positively necessary Campbell's Cream of Mushroom soup. She had been in the H.E.B. for two and a half hours. Well, thirty minutes was a brief conversation with Wanda Stewart about her unfortunate daughter who was trying to become a singer and moved to crazy Austin. And, Ginny had even brought a list. She was almost home, but Ginny pulled into the Odessa Church of Christ parking lot, turned her Saturn around, and headed back to the market. "You can't have Christmas dinner without three bean casserole," Ginny thought. And, as Ginny drove back to the H.E.B., she let her mind roll to what else she had forgotten. Growing older had not been the joyride to grace her mother, may she rest in peace, had promised.

*****

Oddly enough, Sam Kitchens was driving to the same H.E.B. feeling very happy and spry, despite the fact and unbeknownst to him, his mission was much the same as Ginny's.

Sam was getting the "fixins," as he was fond of calling them, for Christmas dinner and he had been planning for it for weeks. The funny part, at least funny to Sam, was that he didn't mind at all that later in his life, after his beloved Christine had passed seven years ago, he had become the master chef for his family. Heck, at 72, Sam no longer was fit to drill in the fields. And, if the truth be known, he did not miss it one bit. Christine, bless her heart, used to smile after he walked in and say, "Sam, you stink worse than a hog on a bad day." But, then, Christine would smile, wash his clothes, send him off to the shower and yell, "But I know how to put lipstick on a pig." He sure missed Christine and still thanked God the cancer took her fast. But, Sam still had a mess of kids, grandkids and former comrades from the oil patch who kept him hopping. Sam did think he would be given a special place in heaven for watching way too many Disney videos with his niece Gloria's kids; but, it was a small price to pay for adoration and, more importantly, for an audience who would listen to him with rapt attention.

Sam wasn't sure exactly how much his cooking had evolved. Sam had always been good at cooking large slabs of red meat to perfection on the grill. But, after Christine died, Sam violated one small promise he made to her and got cable. Sam immediately became a food channel junkie. Sam attributed this current obsession to Emeril, who Sam thought was a "man's man" and even though he talked funny, he sure was enthusiastic about his work. Cooking was much like drilling for oil. Sometimes, if you worked hard enough at it, amazing and wonderful things could come out of the ground or the oven. And, more often than you'd care to admit, you could work all day and end up with a complete, total disaster. Sam actually wrote Emeril to find out what went wrong with that veal dish which, when Sam got through it, resembled beef jerky. But, fortunately, only Sam had been there to eat it and Sam very much liked beef jerky. Never had jerky with a veal-like flavor before.

Christmas dinner really was for Sam's four daughters; Ruby, Crystal, Jade and Jackie, each of whom Sam loved beyond life itself. Sam always wondered whether he was slightly closer to Jackie because she was the youngest or because she was the only child not named after some type of rock. Sam and Christine never figured out where the rock thing came from, but once they started with it you just don't fix things if they ain't broke. But, for reasons that Sam could never understand, Christine had always worshipped Jackie Kennedy and when the last one came along Christine had said, "Let's stop doing rocks. She looks just like Jackie." And so the name stuck.

Sam understood completely, although he never said it out loud, that his daughters supported his cooking addiction and especially Christmas dinner because it "kept him busy." His daughters even ordered exotic kitchen utensils for him off the Internet from Williams Sonoma. Half the time, Sam could not figure out what the device was for; but, he religiously hung up each new one in his kitchen. Privately, Sam was hoping for a new sweater from Jade instead of the usual four new utensils.

None of this mattered at this special moment. The heater was working in his little Toyota, he was two minutes away from the H.E.B., and the only question was how was he going to navigate two full shopping carts. Sam saw the light turn green and was thinking about his special oyster dressing for the turkey. Sam was halfway through the intersection with the H.E.B. in sight when everything changed forever.

*****

What else had she forgotten, Ginny thought, as she glanced down at her list on the passenger seat.

As she glanced back up, she saw her light had turned red, but she was already through it. She saw the car just ahead, a small one, a man, a full head of white hair, and then everything moved so fast but in slow motion. A horrible, terrible smash and the sound of crashing metal and breaking glass. Ginny hurtled toward the windshield but her seatbelt held.

She thought she saw the man's face before everything went black. She thought she heard sirens and someone asking her questions.

Hours later, Ginny woke up in a hospital bed, her husband and children around her. Bill, her husband and one of the few remaining good family doctors in Odessa, was holding Ginny's hand and jumped up when Ginny's eyes opened.

"You gave us all quite a scare," Bill said. "How are you feeling?"

Ginny tried to manage words but she realized she was almost choking on tears that were seemingly rolling down her throat.

"You don't need to speak, Ginny," Bill said. "You're banged up some, but you are going to be all right."

Ginny summoned whatever strength she had and gently tugged Bill closer to her.

"The man?" she breathed. "The man?"

"He didn't make it, dear. He didn't make it," Bill said.

Ginny heard the words and prayed that this was some terrible dream. Mercifully, Ginny fell back asleep. When she woke again the next morning in the same hospital bed, Ginny realized it was not simply a terrible dream and something deep inside told her the nightmare was just beginning.

*****

Ginny reflected on that terrible December day today; but, it was two years later and she glanced at Bill who was driving her in their Navigator to Austin. Reflecting back was pretty much all Ginny had done both before, during and after physical therapy. The fact that it was December made it probably worse. Ginny had come to almost hate Christmas and felt its cold press around Halloween. Christmas was, as always, speeding down the rails; but, now she was lying on the track like in one of those old movies with no hope of escape. Sure, she had met her share of heroic rescuers. The best psychologists, pastoral counselors, and potent anti-depressants had done their level best to unbind the ropes and save the day. But, the mighty Christmas train had her in its sights and Papa Noel wasn't blowing any whistle.

Objectively, if Ginny had any capacity to be objective, Ginny was a complete and total disaster. She had not been behind the wheel since what everyone now referred to as "the accident" and could barely get in a car, even when dependable Bill was driving. Ginny had dropped thirty pounds because depression, she had been advised, had robbed her of her appetite. Bill kept telling Ginny she looked great, but she had, without exception, refused him any hope of intimacy. She slept poorly, but now refused the pills. Ginny had other new addictions. She didn't need the pills.

The need to reflect back on "the accident" seemed especially important today. They were driving to Austin to attend a mediation to end what was now referred to as "the lawsuit" which resulted from "the accident."

Initially, Ginny felt modest relief that she wasn't going to jail although the largest part of her spirit believed that is where she belonged. Ginny, like everyone back home, didn't like to sugarcoat things. The equation was terribly simple. I didn't pay attention. I ran a red light at an intersection I have crossed a zillion times. I killed a man. I killed a very good, kind, vital man. What else was there to say?

And, today, at this mediation thing, I am going to see his precious daughters whom I have never met and have never spoken to even though we live in the same place, probably less than four miles from each other.

That part of it all was the most baffling to Ginny. After Ginny was in the clear, Ginny wanted to call and visit the family. But, her brother the lawyer and the lawyer her insurance company had hired to represent her in "the lawsuit" told her there could be no contact with the other family. Ginny was reminded there could be criminal charges and even, if not, she would surely be sued. Anything Ginny could say could and would be used against her. Her lawyer brother seemed to almost enjoy reminding her "you never listened to anyone before, but this time you just have to keep your mouth shut."

Ginny thought all that was indecent and it certainly was not very Christian; but, everything about this had become indecent. Ginny had told her insurance lawyer that the company should give the family whatever they want. Her lawyer told Ginny it just didn't work that way but hopefully everything would get settled at mediation. Ginny's lawyer told her that he would do most of the talking at mediation and that the mediator was there to help everyone arrive at "a number" that would settle "the lawsuit."

Talking about "a number" made Ginny sick. Whether mediation was about numbers or about something else, Ginny spent most her time thinking what she could possibly say to Ruby, Crystal, Jade and Jackie, now collectively referred to as "the plaintiffs." Ginny tried to put herself in their shoes. What would they be thinking? Ginny knew what she would be thinking. Some ditsy doctor's wife wasn't paying attention and killed our father and she should pay for it.

Bill pulled the car into a space next to the mediation center by the lake. Ginny's lawyer was already there along with an insurance company representative. As Ginny was escorted into a private room that was going to be "their room," she peered through the glass and saw four women and a man, their law-

yer, Ginny guessed, seated on one side of the conference table. "The daughters," Ginny said out loud as
she felt her stomach tighten.

*****

Jackie glanced up as Ginny walked by. She had
been wanting to finally get a look at this woman.
Jackie saw Ginny look in and it felt as if every bit
of her breath had been sucked out. Jackie had been
waiting for this very moment. She needed to see the
woman who had killed her beloved father.

Jackie was the involuntary spokesperson and decision-maker for her sisters. Ruby had not wanted
to file a lawsuit and had told her sisters "Lawsuits
don't raise the dead." Crystal and Jade hadn't felt
much different but all had succumbed to Jackie's
plea, "We've got to do this for dad. We've got to
make this right." In moments of sadness and reflection, none of this felt exactly right to Jackie. Jeff,
their lawyer and a certifiably good guy, had done a
full investigation of Virginia Stevens. The report, in
a tabbed and indexed binder, told the whole story.
No prior traffic accidents. Two speeding tickets in
the past twenty years. Amazing by West Texas stan-
dards. No drugs or alcohol on the day of the accident. No history of drugs or alcohol. Large history
of charitable work, volunteer work in the schools,
working at a food shelter, and even a volunteer at
the rape crisis center. Regularly attends the other

Methodist church. No speeding when the accident occurred. Just missed the red light. Virtually admitted the mistake to the police. The mistake that killed my father.

Jackie had been infuriated that Ginny had never tried to contact the family or even send a card until Jeff told her that her lawyers would advise against it and never allow her to do it. "Well, the law sort of stinks on that one, Jeff," Jackie said. Jeff just winked and shrugged his shoulders. Nice guy, never an unkind word about anyone.

As much time as Jackie had spent thinking about the mediation, she never felt less prepared and more uncertain about what she would do. Jeff had provided a full explanation of what mediation was and what might happen. But, Jeff also said "Mediation is also really different and sometimes weird things happen." Jackie actually liked the different part but found "weird things" to be somewhat unsettling. Jackie remembered saying a prayer on Sunday that things go well today. She didn't really know what "go well" meant. Christmas was coming soon and each Christmas since Dad had passed seemed to weigh ever heavier on her heart. It wasn't something she could put her finger on precisely.

Jackie, and her sisters too, still mourned the fact they did not have a chance to say goodbye to their father. Dad, according to the doctors, had died instantly; "sort of like a bug hitting your windshield when you're driving 90," said one of the obviously compassionate physicians. Crystal often commented "at least Dad didn't suffer" and Jade would remind them "he led a vital, healthy life and he went out strong." Sometimes, Jackie found some consolation in such thoughts; but, the plain truth was that Dad didn't need to die and she wasn't ready for him to die.

The oddest thing, at least by Jackie's way of thinking, is that even though Dad had been laid to rest years ago, she didn't feel as if he was buried. Letters from her lawyer, hearing dates, depositions, and now this mediation thing – all of it felt, when she opened some chatty letter from Jeff, like it was just happening. While Jackie ostensibly was back at work and back to being a mom and better than average wife, Jackie felt like her life was somehow on hold. Jackie had little reason to believe today would make things different; but she really hoped that might be so. Dad used to call Jackie "the hope of our family." Sometimes he used the word "glue." Jackie liked "hope" better; but she understood that for reasons she couldn't fully explain that her father bestowed captain of the family ship status on the youngest. Dad said it had everything to do with her heart.

Jackie was hoping at this moment she could find it.

*****

The next thing Ginny remembered is that some-how she must have sleepwalked into a large confer-ence room. She was sitting at a table with her hus-band and lawyer next to her. The daughters were less than three feet across the table from her with their lawyer. She could almost reach out and touch them. She wanted to look at each of them straight in the eye, the West Texas way; but, she could only glance from time to time.

The mediator, dressed a little funny, but apparent-ly caring, made a presentation. The tone was com-forting but Ginny did not hear many of his words. Next, the daughters' lawyer spoke very briefly. He seemed kind, almost nice. Ginny wanted to hear of the four women speak. The mediator encouraged them to speak; but, they didn't. Ginny's counsel told her their lawyer would tell them not to speak; but, Ginny was disappointed anyway. Even if their words were harsh, cruel or condemning, it would have been better. Ginny had it coming.

Ginny's thoughts were disrupted by hearing her own lawyer's words. Ginny was sure she heard her lawyer say, "we're sorry." Ginny thought that must be said but she almost resented her lawyer saying it for her. Then there were details about "the accident." Ginny tuned out her own lawyer until she began to hear him talk about her suffering. "You know," her lawyer said to the four women, "my client has been clinically depressed since the accident, has been on medication, and has virtually become a recluse." Ginny's lawyer added more words and then stated, "You know Ginny has never been behind the wheel of a car since the accident."

Sometimes when the fortunes and fates are right in West Texas, the drill hits a special spot in which the physical force becomes so powerful that it blows away all in its black wake. Something like that welled up in Ginny's soul – an irresistible, unstoppable force of amazing clarity.

"This has nothing to do with me or whether I can drive or how badly I am feeling. How dare anyone talk about me?" Ginny blurted. The room fell silent.

"This is about," said Ginny, looking across the table, straight into the eyes of each of the four women, "what I did to your father."

"God forgive me," Ginny said. "I wasn't paying attention. I have wound and rewound what happened a thousand times. I keep asking myself why? Why was I thinking about Christmas dinner instead of driving? What was so important? Why did I look down? It was just for a half a second. And then the red light. I saw the white hair. I think I saw his face. It was all my fault. I didn't mean it to happen. I didn't want it to happen. I've never hurt anyone before. I've learned what a great and wonderful man he was. I am so very, very sorry. I would gladly trade places with your father if I could. I have caused your family such terrible harm. Not meaning or intending it is no excuse. But, I'm sorry for all the pain…and all the unimaginable heartache I have caused you."

Ginny's words seemed to echo off the walls into the church quiet of the room. Sometimes silence is uncomfortable. Sometimes silence is necessary. The room felt like it had moved someplace else. Where it was no one really knew.

Certainty and clarity, sometimes elusive, may find you at the strangest times. Something, something beyond labeling, found Jackie. Jackie looked at the mediator and between her own tears asked, "Are Ginny and I allowed to be alone together?" The mediator answered affirmatively and Jackie got up, went around the table, and softly touched Ginny on the shoulder. Ginny got up and, guided by Jackie, went into a room and shut the door.

*****

Jackie and Ginny were in the room alone for over two hours. With regrets to drama and theatre, the words and feelings exchanged between Jackie and Ginny belong uniquely and solely to them.

There was no Speilberg music when they walked out, arm in arm, and for those who witnessed the moment, it did not feel that way. On this day, Jackie felt Dad was finally at peace. Ginny had expressed sorrow and responsibility and without seeking or requesting it had received forgiveness. Dad's hope, the family's hope, had recognized that two families had become inextricably intertwined because of a terrible moment in time. Dad's hope was that Jackie would always find a way to forgive, to heal, and to restore. Jackie always felt that obligation applied to her own family. But today, for reasons that Jackie felt made no objective sense, her family had grown somewhat larger. Ginny and Bill would have Christmas dinner with Jackie's family this year. And Jackie, with Ginny's help, would cook some of Dad's favorite recipes and use all those utensils that had now found their way into her kitchen. In a way, this was an ending and a beginning. Much healing was left to be done. Not everything was neat and tidy and safe and maybe it would never be completely. But just as the West Texas weather can turn on a dime and change on you, something in that large West Texas way had changed – something that would likely grow in the retelling.

When they came out of the room, all Jackie said was "We're going home."

Ginny looked at Jackie and said, "That's right, we're going home. So, the two women left and headed west. Christmas was coming and it would be here soon.

Chapter 11

On Change and Reinvention

Mediators can and do settle into routines. After twenty or thirty mediations, mediators discover things that work, develop approaches that feel comfortable, and without knowing it, become predictable.

This phenomenon makes sense. Recall your first ten mediations. You were tentative. You felt the floor would open up and you would fall in. You felt powerless, alone, and inwardly scared as hell. No one likes that feeling of insecurity and vulnerability; but you got through it in one piece and even managed to settle most of those disputes. Suddenly, you feel a bit more comfortable.

Your mediator's introduction becomes natural and effective. Your questioning techniques improve. You begin to actually feel you know what to do in a private caucus. You find you are beginning to enjoy being a mediator. The work remains as challenging; but, you are less stressed out and far more confident. Thirty or forty mediations later, you begin to think you've got everything figured out. And someone once told you, you don't fix something if it's not broken. I know this is not terribly profound, but all I can say is "uh-oh." I know what I am about to say will not resonate with all of you; but, I believe that the most necessary changes occur at the moment of perceived success. I believe that a mediator should transform and reinvent himself at least every other year.

Predictability is the curse of any mediator. A mediator must constantly add new techniques and methods. The greatest complement someone may give you is that you have never approached a mediation exactly the same way. Each time you are different and equally effective. Your market has not figured you out and that is a very good thing. You don't fit in a predictable mediator's slot. You are not like everyone else. People begin to view you as an artist; as being in a different place.

How exactly does a mediator reinvent himself? I think the first step is a philosophical commitment to the concept that mediations are like snowflakes-they are all a bit different. As such, a mediator must adjust and also be different.

You might begin reinvention with the basics, those things you already do well. Your mediator's introduction is a good start.

After fifty to a hundred renditions, your introduction may sound good; but it may come across as scripted, something you could deliver in your sleep. Also, some people may have by now heard your mediator's introduction five or six times; usually, the lawyers.

Keep in mind that your mediator's introduction is for the parties, the people. The parties need to hear your introduction and it is the first building block in trust building. Your introduction, beneath its formative content, is designed to humanize and explain a process that is strange and mysterious to first time users. People will not become engaged in a process in which they feel uncomfortable. I think mediators tend to gloss over words which are powerful, unusual, and not readily understood by many people. I am thinking of the words neutrality, confidentiality, risk, delay, cost, and closure. Such words, when you think about them, are not things that most people deal with or use on a daily basis.

For example, neutrality is not an easy concept for most people and many people view neutrality as a horribly unnatural state of being. People live, especially in these times, in a horribly judgmental world. Employers, friends, the media, colleagues, and the list goes on, are frequently judgmental. The parties at mediation are frequently judgmental themselves.

The parties, looking at you, a total stranger, may fail to believe or trust that you could be neutral. The parties don't know you. The parties have never met anyone like you. When was the last time a total stranger promised you he would be neutral? Would you believe it? A good explanation of neutrality presents a wonderful opportunity for a mediator to differentiate the mediation process from normal world experiences. You are, through your explanation, transporting parties to a very special place.

Confidentiality is an equally powerful concept; but, also in a world of gossip and disclosure something people are not used to. In terms of reinvention, consider doing more than describing or promising confidentiality. Explain the impact of confidentiality and how, as with neutrality, confidentiality creates a different world.

Risk is also another powerful word in your mediator's introduction. Mediators often simply advise the parties that mediations allows all sides to avoid the risk of trial. But, what exactly does that mean to the average participant? Not much. We understand risk and that most people are risk adverse. Behavioral studies in negotiation demonstrates such risk aversion time and time again.

Participants at mediation need more help in visualizing risk, not in order to terrify them, but in order to motivate them to seize the opportunity mediation affords. The average participant has never risked $50,000.00 in the stock market, on a real estate investment, or in a casino. The average participant will almost always keep a $1000.00 sure thing than reaching in a bin of envelopes and having a one in four chance of winning $5000.00. Many people assess risks based on perceived odds, i.e. what are my statistical objective chances of winning a hand of black jack. Many people who have taken risks have lost; or, they have had friends who have experienced losses.

In court-annexed mediations, the risks inherent in a trial are almost off the chart. The only certainty is that lawyers will not warrant an outcome for a client. In a friendly way at mediation, ask a lawyer to execute a written warranty his client will receive no less than $100,000.00 through trial and appeal. I sometimes ask this question politely and discretely when a lawyer says, "My client is only netting $200,000.00 with the amount the other side if offering." Forgive me; but, I can't juxtapose only and $200,000.00 in the same sentence. I think most people would have a similar problem.

If you tried lawsuits as I did, describing the risks of a trial is fairly easy. You might briefly insinuate and describe these risks in your introduction. I especially like describing risks which will resonate with participants on a visceral level.

For example jurors and judges are complete and total strangers. You are allowing complete and total strangers to decide your fate,

Or you don't know who the jurors or judge will be. At least you know that a deck of cards has 52 cards and you also know what each card is and what each card is worth. With a jury you don't know who will show up or what they will think.

One other thing is certain about trials; there will not be 12 people exactly like you on the jury.

Another way to help the parties feel risk is describing how lawyers feel, despite their confidence, after the jurors go in to the jury room, shut the door and begin to deliberate. That moment is terribly unsettling for lawyers and they will admit it. Why is this so unsettling? This leads to another powerful word that may be insinuated into your mediator's introduction and thought process.

Is there something people fear even worse than risk? How about loss of control? The reason a lawyer's stomachs drop when jurors close the door is that is the moment all control is lost. Trial is abdicating control and decision making to total strangers. More positively stated, mediation gives you, the party control, over your own outcome and you have a direct hand in creating a resolution.

Control equals ownership. Most people prefer anything they control or own and also believe they know what they need better than total strangers ever will. Ownership, often a neglected word in a mediator's lexicon, is an extremely powerful symbol.

Why? People take pride in things they own. People stick with and trust things they own. People are interested and believe in things they own. The parties own the mediation process. The parties have ownership in the decision-making. Ownership also implies responsibility. You may not expect first time or occasional users of the process to know or understand these things. You must tell them.

Most people fear risk. Most people dislike loss of control. Most people also hate delay- in almost every facet of their lives. People don't like to stand in lines, to be kept waiting by their doctor or lawyer, or suffer an airplane rescheduling. Many mediators suggest that in mediation we can avoid delay. But, what does that mean to people inexperienced with the civil justice system? The delay needs to be more specifically described; i.e. trial and appeal in this venue might take three to four years. Most people are simply not used to that type of delay. Three of four years might be a lifetime for many people. Most people do not wish to wait four years to solve a problem.

The more positive description, described as a comparison, is that mediation involves many people's favorite words; i.e. <u>today</u> and <u>now</u>. We can achieve a resolution <u>today</u>! The more specific description of these concepts creates an initial buy-in and momentum in favor of the mediation process. Most people prefer to live in a world in which things get done quickly.

Cost is also an underutilized word. Cost usually is defined as attorney's fees or expense. But, the litigation process exacts a more terrible cost, i.e. the human toll that conflict and the system has on people. Conflict carries with it an emotional cost that is very difficult to evaluate. Emotional strife may and often does have an economic price. What would be the price of either damaging or improving your piece of mind?

Cost, more broadly defined, becomes the prelude to closure, something the process has a great potential to offer. Closure is not a readily understood word. Many people do not know what closure means.

Mediators need to be careful with the word closure. The word may be misunderstood. Closure does not mean feeling better right away. Closure does not mean "healed." Closure is the pathway which allows people to feel better and begin the healing process.

Many people hunger for closure and the opportunity to feel better and heal. The stress associated with a conflict or dispute may exact a great personal and emotional toll on the people involved. The possibility of closure is a beacon light that will sustain them throughout a mediation. Its power should not be underestimated.

Another facet of reinvention may also involve improving questioning techniques and thereby better engaging the parties.

Fledgling mediators often think of boatloads of fact intensive questions. Inundating a party with a battery of factual questions often is counterproductive. Facts at mediation are like quicksand; i.e. everyone may easily get buried by the facts.

Interestingly, experienced mediators improve their questioning techniques by moving from the complex and detailed to the most basic questions. A simple open-ended question regarding feelings will usually produce a flood of information and immediately engage the parties. The most sublime and most difficult part of questioning is knowing when to stop talking. If you ask a good question, follow your own rules; i.e. listen and do not interrupt. The responses to a good question become the texts to many other conversations- if you do not interrupt the flow of information.

Another enhancement of questioning is do not rush a party to the cliff. Permit me to explain. Assume that you are aware that the party with whom you are sitting has authored a series of emails that are terribly damaging to his position. Further assume that you are in private caucus. Also assume that you believe that if the party reflects objectively on the impact of the emails that a re-evaluation will occur.

In this hypothetical, the emails are the cliff. The party knows he wrote the emails. The party also may know the emails hurt his position. The party probably does not want to believe just how damaging the emails are. The party is also likely waiting for a question about the emails and is planning on what to say about them. The emails terrify this party.

A remarkably effective technique is also to create a safe environment in which the party brings up the emails. Such a technique requires patience and trust building by the mediator. Ultimately, you want the party to say "I suppose you'll want to talk with me about those emails?" Suddenly the emails become an invited conversation and invited discussions are less frightening. Also, your response to the invitation does not have to be a question. Your response might simply be "I'd be happy to discuss the emails." You then stop and wait. The party will almost always clue you in on how he feels comfortable talking about this matter. Your goal of course is to provide a safe path for the party to reach his own conclusions about the emails. The only difference is that the party now has a safe companion along for the ride.

This essay is not a dissertation on questioning techniques. My point is that a mediator at any stage of her practice should periodically ask, "Do I ask questions well and might I be able to do it better?" If you are finding you are not consistently engaging the parties, you might first take a hard look at your questioning techniques.

Re-invention and change involves in essence a sort of check- up. A self- assessment check-up is possible; but, for obvious reasons, not entirely reliable. The better practice is to find someone you trust uniquely and whose opinion you respect and ask them to observe you during a mediation. Your trusted friend must be encouraged to be entirely candid and specific. You must be truly willing to receive your trusted friend's input. You will learn many things, almost all of which will allow you to make necessary adjustments.

Re-invention and change helps keep you fresh and the process fresh. You become less predictable, more invigorated, and most important, a better mediator.

Chapter 12

On Mediators' Styles

"Ch-ch-ch-ch changes"
Changes, David Bowie

Since the dawn of the modern mediation revolution, experts have tried to label and define every aspect of the process. Mediators have not been exempt from these efforts and some experts have determined that mediators have different "styles."

These experts have used terms such as "facilitative," "evaluative," "active or proactive," and "passive" to describe mediators' styles, frequently rendering opinions whether certain mediator styles or behaviors are really mediation at all. I must confess a bias against too much labeling or defining mediation. Mediation is a flexible, fluid, creative process-virtually indefinable in my opinion. And I also must confess after sixteen years of mediation I do not know what my style is. I do know I do not have a single style. Once, ten years ago, I wrote in another book that mediators are chameleon-like; i.e., mediators adjust their "styles" to the particular dispute and personalities they are working with. I still am convinced that remains true.

Every mediator or peacemaker brings his or her personality to the practice of mediation. You don't cease to be yourself when you become a mediator and being true to yourself will probably make you a better mediator.

But, of course, you have to know who you are. Sometimes we think or hope we know. Some feedback often helps. I have often wondered why a personality assessment is not part of mediation training. One would think, after all, that certain dominant personality characteristics might be reliable predictors as to whether someone likely will or will not be an effective mediator.

For example, certain people and personalities are terribly judgmental. I have a difficult time believing that a dominantly judgmental person may consistently and reliably suspend the tendency to be judgmental simply because they are acting as a mediator. A terribly judgmental personality will have an exceedingly difficult time with neutrality and many other aspects of the process.

On the other hand, certain personalities not only accept but relish diversity. For such personalities, people and their differences are a real turn-on. One would think, barring any other negative characteristics, that people who relish diversity would be superior mediators. Unless, of course, such people judge people harshly who do not accept diversity.

If patience is an essential quality of a mediator, how will a personality which is inherently impatient at work, at home, with friends, and with the world in general fare as a mediator? I guess I believe you can't fake a personality characteristic you don't actually possess. If a disputant is pouring his heart out to you and you are inwardly thinking "can't we get beyond this," the disputant will know that is exactly what you are thinking or feeling. So I suppose that a mediator really needs to know who he or she is and the impact his or her personality has on other people.

Often, we determine the impact of our personalities based on our perceptions of what our friends think about us; but, I think, probably unconsciously, we select people who will find our personalities agreeable or, at the very least, tolerable.

Assume for the moment you have a pretty good handle on who you are and how people react to you. Assume further, you possess many of the qualities a mediator must possess. The real kicker may be that your personality may not match up well with the personalities of certain disputants.

This reality, I believe, is what the issue of mediation styles is really about and why I suggest good mediators are chameleon-like.

For example, I know I am an extremely extroverted, often passionate, person. I like to break through barriers quickly. I am willing to open up easily and gravitate to people who are willing to do the same. I love people and believe diversity truly rocks. I am not terribly controlling, but I can be pushy at times. My face is very expressive and I know certain reactions may be read. I have a small inner core that no one gets to see and very few even know about; but, I think (hope) that's true of everyone.

Some of these personality characteristics make me a very effective mediator. But, some of these personality characteristics may clash with certain people unless I am extremely careful.

For example, I know that I may make a very quiet, introverted person very uncomfortable if I unleash the personality my friends find moderately entertaining. A stranger's handshake, eye contact, demeanor, tone of voice, and body language provides much information. If I am thinking that a disputant is very passive, I know I have to adjust my tone; or, if you like the chameleon metaphor, adjust my color. The chameleon is still a chameleon whether it's blue, black, brown, yellow, or green. And, you are still you even with an adjustment of tone.

With the passive person, I am inwardly telling myself to go slow, do not push too hard, be especially patient, be gentle, and allow this person the space and opportunity to reach out to you.

What makes this aspect of mediation so sublimely interesting is that you may have an exact opposite personality in the other room. The other disputant is extroverted, extremely candid, and just wants to get down to business as quickly as possible. Assume this is a personality that matches up very well with yours and inside you are thinking "Thank goodness, I can just be myself."

You are likely already sniffing at another dimension of the personality styles issue. Do we consciously or unconsciously gravitate at mediation towards personalities that are better matches with our own, and, if so, does this impact neutrality? Or, if neutrality is not affected, do personality mismatches impact other aspects of the process? Would a mediator spend more time with the party most like them? Does a mediator become frustrated because a more passive party will not bond with them?

I don't know the answers to these questions; but, I raise them to promote the elevated level of awareness necessary to assess whether these issues factor into what you do at any level.

Assuming your personality is not affecting neutrality, a mediator's challenge is to rather quickly assess many personalities and make appropriate internal personality adjustments to play the type of music which everyone will find at least comfortable. Such necessary adjustments explain why mediators may move in and out of different "styles" during the course of the same mediation.

Disputant's needs, moods, and desires do not remain static during a mediation. Disputant's needs, wants and desires often change, sometimes dramatically, during the process. Initially, a disputant may want or need simply a good listener. That same disputant, later in the process, may need someone more directive and may actually request more input. Mediators sometimes makes these transformations consciously; and, sometimes unconsciously.

But, "styles" is a rather simplistic way of describing a more sublime and challenging process.

Perhaps a better way of describing this phenomenon is that mediators constantly make adjustments during a process which is inherently flexible. Such adjustments may be large or small; but, mediators will likely make dozens, if not hundreds, of adjustments during a mediation.

Mediators, while very intuitive, are not telepathic. Judgment calls about personality is tricky business and a mediator's initial assessments may be wrong. Thus, the constant need to adjust. Happily, a few constants do exist. Caring is a constant. Dedication, perseverance, tenacity, and patience are also constants. Disputants, if these constants are present, will adjust along with the mediator because such constants create and build trust.

In the end, capable mediators live in the moment, ears to the ground, and adjusting to the new realities in which they find themselves.

Chapter 13

On Assumptions

"When I first saw you, I thought you were handsome; then, of course, you spoke."
Carol Connelly in As Good as it Gets

"There are two types of people in this world: those who like Neil Diamond, and those who don't."
Bob Wiley in What About Bob

Assumptions are what we think or believe to be true without having all the information. All human beings, by nature, assume many things. We assume how certain people will act, what they will feel, what is true, and what is important and what is not important. Sometimes, our assumptions are right. But, more frequently, our assumptions are wrong. People can and do surprise us. Actually, people are surprising us because we have assumed too much, or assumed incorrectly.

Mediators, more than anybody, must be aware of and careful about assumptions. Assumptions become artificial roadblocks. Assumptions are creatures of our own invention. There must be a mantra somewhere to help us with assumptions because assumptions get in the way. Perhaps we create artificial impasses because we assume too much. Some of it is the disputant's baggage. But, how much baggage do we bring to the table?

So here's a mantra to add to our repertoires. Paradigms do not exist here. So this is a beginning. You create an ending and modify as you deem fit.

1.   What is unimportant to me may be very important to you.

2.   What is important to me may be unimportant to you.

3.   I will, under no circumstance, assume my beliefs, values, and perceptions are valued or shared by the disputant.

4.   I will not assume I know what a disputant feels.

5.   I will not assume I understand how a disputant feels.

6.   I will not assume I know what an appropriate settlement should be.

7.   I will not assume because of job title or professional status how a person will behave or feel.

8.   I will not assume based on cultural, religious, ethnic, socioeconomic or political

bases how a person will behave or feel or what is or what is not important to them.

9. I will not assume what the disputant's hopes or expectations of the mediation process are without asking them.

10. I will not assume non-monetary interests are of no value or are of great value without exploring such issues with the disputants.

11. I will not assume after reading pre-mediation submissions whether the case is likely or unlikely to settle.

12. I will not assume I know what a dispute is really about based on what I have read in advance of the mediation session.

13. I will not assume I know what is driving or fueling a dispute solely based on the remarks of lawyers in the joint session.

14. I will not assume the lawyers know what is truly important to their own clients.

15. I will not assume that based on my mediator's introduction that the disputants trust me.

16. I will not assume that lawyers have adequately or accurately prepared their clients for the mediation process.

17. I will not assume that disputants, whether represented or not, fully understand the mediation process or the mediator's role.

18. I will not assume that an apology does or does not matter.

19. I will not assume whether disputants do or do not desire a future personal, professional, or business relationship.

20. I will not assume a disputant is or is not reasonable based solely on their behavior during the process.

21. I will not assume that any aspect of a dispute is trivial or insignificant.

22. I will not assume I know how a lawyer wishes for you to interact with his client without asking.

23. I will not assume that opening offers during a session or indicative of how each side values a dispute.

24. I will not assume that declarations of what a disputant will never do are necessarily true or untrue.

25. I will not assume that a final offer is in fact a final offer until it's finality is tested.

26. I will not assume that the parties or their lawyers are necessarily being candid with you or telling you the whole story.

27. I will not assume after viewing pre-mediation submissions or hearing opening statements that you understand the dispute better than people who have been involved with it for months or years.

As I mentioned, the list is only a partial list and more of an illustration of the types of assumption even experienced mediators can and do make. A mediator's assumption or assumptions, if incorrect, may actually create an unnecessary or false impasse.

Effective questioning techniques prevent incorrect assumptions. Mediators often feel the press of time and the need to move the process along. Appropriate information gathering does involve substantial amounts of time; but, a mediator needs to devote enough time to be certain he knows, and does not simply assume, what truly does or does not matter to the disputants.

Chapter 14

On Loneliness

"There's a lotta things about me
you don't know anything about, Dottie.
Things you wouldn't understand. Things
you couldn't understand."
Pee Wee Herman in Pee Wee's Big Adventure

Despite their passion for the process and the great fulfillment peacemakers often feel, mediators occasionally feel a profound sense of loneliness. I have felt this and too many mediators have expressed this feeling to me after a few glasses of wine for me to believe this to be an uncommon experience. Why do mediators feel lonely? And what should mediators do about this?

I think the greatest reason mediators feel a sense of loneliness is because they come to believe that no one understands what they do or feel, except for other mediators. Even worse, mediators sometimes perceive that the people they interact with think their jobs are easy. Mediators who interact with attorneys may hear a glib remark like "You get paid the big bucks for this?" Interestingly, the true parties to a mediation rarely believe a mediator's task is easy. How often have you heard a party say "You mean you actually do this everyday?" Nothing about the practice of mediation is easy. A mediator, using both sides of his brain, must make dozens of spontaneous process and people decisions. Sometimes objective realities dictate such decision-making. Far more often, a mediator relies on gut, instinct, and intuition in making a critical process decision. And, sometimes these process decisions are not immediately understood by the participants and may even create some temporary discomfort. If you asked a mediator why she made an important process decision immediately after she made it, a mediator may not be able to fully explain it. Experience, a sense of people, a feeling of what is right, and a degree of fearlessness (not recklessness) all play in the decision. An experienced mediator, either consciously or unconsciously is already planning what to do if the decision is wrong or where to go if the decision turned out to be right.

The mediator in essence is walking a tight rope without a net, constantly in danger of falling into the abyss. The mediator is up there in lights for all to see... alone.

Unlike almost anything else, mediators do not receive cheers or support for good process decisions.

Often the participants do not understand the significance of the decision or realize that the mediator is holding his breath to see what happens. In baseball, a pitcher may pitch nine innings. If the pitcher strikes out the side in the fifth inning by insinuating a slider or an off speed pitch into his repertoire, the crowd goes wild. But, the crowd understands pitching and its nuances. And, the pitcher has a defensive team behind him. When the pitcher gets the last batter out in the ninth, the fans and the media will proclaim the pitcher's fastball was really on and he was really spotting his pitches.

Of course, none of this applies to mediators. A mediator might make thirty to fifty different "pitches," i.e. process decisions, during a mediation. But, the mediator usually is the only one who knows what those pitches were and what he did, albeit fatigued, to survive the last three innings.

The punch line of course, is that the mediator, due to confidentiality, doesn't get to talk about it. The case either did or did not settle. But, the perilous journey towards resolution, with its emotional peaks and valleys, is known only to the mediator and probably, if told; only understood by other mediators.

To be sure, the process belongs to the parties and the parties make the magic. And, experienced mediators do not feel the compulsion to brag or receive accolades. Most experienced mediators feel a profound sense of relief that somehow things worked out and an internal sense of pride that certain process decisions turned out to be correct.

But, when the parties and their counsel leave, the mediator is again alone. A mediator begins, remains, and ends alone.

The spiritual rewards that mediation gives to a mediator make this sense of loneliness endurable and inherent part of the mediator's job. No job is perfect. Everything in life involves trade-offs.

But, the loneliness of a mediator's life must be acknowledged because through acknowledgement loneliness does not transform into a larger more toxic problem and because a mediator will also discover he is not as alone as he thinks.

Mediators must seek out the company of other mediators not only for the education that collaboration brings; but, for the sheer companionship of being around similarly situated professionals. A mediator will find that he has new friends in Cleveland, New York, Seattle, Miami, or Austin who all feel the same things and go through the same daily journeys. Mediators need to be around people who speak the same language- people who you don't have to explain everything to and who simply understand.

Oddly, I find this aspect of otherwise wonderful mediator seminars to be most lacking. The hundreds of informative and highly educational workshops are essential. But, more opportunities should be available for mediators to share what it feels like to be a mediator; i.e. a mediators hopes, fears concerns, worries and also a sharing of triumphs and victories. In short, the caretakers need to be better caretakers of each other and recognize that people who do so much good for others need some nurturing from time to time.

So the next time your mediation ends, everyone leaves at 1:00am, and that lonely feeling creeps under your skin, remember this essay and know you are not alone. Thousands of your colleagues understand what you are feeling. And, if you listen carefully and listen very, very hard, we are cheering wildly about that play you made in extra innings that made resolution possible. You won't read about it in tomorrow's box score; but, you can feel it from our hearts to yours.

Chapter 15

On Mediator Labels

"Who are you? Who, who, who, who?"
Who Are You, The Who

If any profession should avoid labels, mediators should. During the modern, American mediation movement, the term "lawyer mediator" or "attorney mediator" has become part of the mediation lexicon. This essay proposes that the term "attorney mediator" be banished as well as any label other than the word <u>mediator.</u>

We know objectively that the legal profession did not invent mediation, although for the past twenty years the legal profession has laid virtual claim to the mediation practice; especially in the American, court-annexed mediation movement. We also know that a background in law does not necessarily predict whether someone will be an effective mediator.

A law background obviously makes it more likely that a mediator will be able to more easily communicate with and understand lawyers and better understand complex legal issues. But, a law background does not make it more likely that a mediator will communicate better with parties or be especially sensitive to their needs, emotions, and interests. Lawyers are trained to look at problems through the prism of relevancy, admissibility, and procedure. Emotional issues, large and small, may be things lawyers experientially are familiar with; but, lawyers are not trained formally to identify, understand, and manage such issues. A basic 40-hour mediation training does not fill this void.

These observations are not criticisms of mediators who happen to be lawyers. I am a mediator who was a practicing lawyer. I also think it would be remarkably difficult for a mediator with no legal background to deal with and manage lawyers and complex legal issues.

Lawyers also have their own language, a sort of difference between what they say and what they mean. Similarly, a mediator who is a lawyer may be better able to evaluate the risk associated with the litigation. If a mediator has never selected a jury, argued in a difficult judge's court, or had to perfect an appeal, a mediator may have no way of knowing what the most likely outcome will be. Additionally, the process should not be burdened with lawyers having to explain to mediators complex concepts that only years of law practice make clear.

Lawyers like to use mediators who speak their

language, who understand their pain, and who may assist them in dealing with both their own clients and the other lawyers and their clients.

This analysis points to an obvious issue. How important is a mediator's background or formal academic training? I think the basic skills sets for an excellent mediator have as much to do with personality traits as formal background or training.

Regardless of background, a mediator must be patient, nonjudgmental, an excellent communicator, respect diversity, and love and understand people. Without these core traits, a person will probably not mediate effectively. Present mediation training rarely, if ever, assesses these qualities.

Assuming these qualities are present, a person must be committed to learning, studying, and appreciating the mediation process. Personality inventory alone does not make a mediator. Effective mediators make a lifetime commitment to studying and learning about the mediation process. Regardless of the absence of standardization, many mediators will spend hundreds of hours annually doing some form of continuing education, be it self-study, formal classes, or seminars.

My point is that two very important building blocks exist even before you get to a mediator's background or formal education. The most fair way to assess background is that each background brings certain strengths to an otherwise qualified mediator and also creates certain liabilities. For example, a formally trained psychologist may be much more capable of appreciating the emotional issues in a dispute but less able, if the dispute is in litigation, to appreciate legal risk. A mediator with a law degree may fully appreciate legal risk but be lost on the emotional complexities of a dispute. Of course, the mediators described above may be intuitively able or with modest case specific education, be able to manage all issues.

My disdain for labeling is really three fold. First, the labeling implies superiority. Second, the mediation process is inherently flexible, fluid, creative, and virtually defies labeling. Third, and probably most important, labels create barriers, a regrettable thing in what is supposed to be a collaborative profession.

Barriers adversely impact communication and, even more important, learning. Mediators, in my opinion, have much to learn from all formal backgrounds. I suppose I just believe that mediation is inherently multi-disciplinary and that the true realization of the mediation movement will come from drawing on the strengths of all these disciplines. Otherwise, mediation will become static and unnecessarily self-limiting. In fact, I cannot think of a discipline, including some unlikely ones, that does not enrich mediation in some way. Forgive but a very partial list.

1. Psychology. I want, as a mediator, to better understand how people feel, why they feel as they do, how conflict affects their emotional well-beings, and how the process may better serve and meet their needs.

2. Religion. More specifically, how does one's spiritual compass affect their orientation, desire, and way of resolving disputes?

3. Cooking. One of the unlikely backgrounds, I know. Great chefs take ostensibly discordant ingredients and produce things that are better than the sum of the parts. Chefs are creative and think outside of the box. Think about it. Chefs have created literally thousands of ways of cooking chicken. And, chefs learn to meet the needs of a diverse audience. Beyond the food, presentation matters. Chefs are also great crisis managers because something always goes wrong and great chefs navigate around disasters.

4. Law. Lawyers are specifically trained to evaluate risk and manage conflicts. Lawyers, despite advocacy, are disciplined to objectively evaluate issues of responsibility and loss. Lawyers learn to mange the expectations of their clients. Lawyers especially understand the concepts of risk and uncertainty.

5. Engineering. Engineers are both creators and problem solvers. An engineer might think how she might make something better or how might she fix something that is not working as well as it should. Engineers use their analytical brains, but often must think outside the box and be terribly creative. Engineers excel at cause and effect and breaking down large problems into smaller, more manageable component parts.

6. Bartenders. Bartenders often have to be especially good listeners. Bartenders often have to deal with people in emotional crisis. Bartenders almost have to be nonjudgmental and careful with their advice.

7. Jazz musicians. Jazz musicians must be collaborative, flexible, and spontaneous. During a particular song, a jazz musician must be open to what is being created and sometimes move in an unexpected direction.

8. Teachers. Great teachers are excellent communicators. Teachers need to explain often complex concepts in a manner which is understandable. Teachers often need to be good listeners and be aware of the reactions, thoughts and needs of their students. Excellent teachers also empower

their students to succeed and chart their own courses.

I'm certain you will think of literally hundreds of other disciplines which would be enlightening and helpful to mediators and the work mediators do.

But, if nothing else, mediation should be a profession of inclusiveness and diversity. The creativity and excellence a person brings to mediation, regardless of background, should be nurtured and acknowledged. We should not become a profession of engineer mediators, lawyer mediators, or psychologist mediators.

We should simply be mediators.

Chapter 16

On Words Mediators Hear

"Inconceivable!" You keep using that word. I do not think it means what you think it means."
Ingo Montoya in <u>The Princess Bride</u>

Mediators hear certain words and phrases quite often during mediation. I hear the following words or phrases a lot and I would like to discuss what they mean and how to deal with them.

1. Never
2. Always
3. Final
4. Win
5. Lose
6. Good Faith
7. Bad Faith
8. Wasting Time
9. Leaving
10. Impasse

Obviously, you need some context for the first word, <u>never.</u>

> I'll never settle this case. We'll never pay more than $20,000.00. I've never lost a jury trial. Nationwide, we have never lost this type of case. Their Summary Judgment will never be granted. We will never do business together again. We never settle at the first mediation.

Well, you get the idea and I'm certain you've heard the word "never" in many other contexts. And, you never (there I go) believe never really, really means never. In fact you probably believe the speaker means the opposite of never. Do parties or lawyers realize that mediators truly do not believe these words and frequently ignore them? They must not; otherwise parties would never use these words with such frequency. And, hopefully, parties do not know how we translate these words and phrases. Consider the following translations.

> "I'll never settle this case."
> ("I'm dying to settle this case.")

> "We'll never pay more than $20,000."
> ("We're going to pay a whole lot more than $20,000.")

> "I've never lost a jury trial."

("I've never had a jury trial.")

"Nationwide, we have never lost this type of case."
("We have settled all the really bad cases and only tried the two best ones in the most favorable defense venues.")

"Their Summary Judgment will never be granted."
("Unless Judge Stevens, Judge Warner, or Judge Davis hears it.")

"We'll never do business together again."
("Unless we can both make money and this time properly lawyer up our deal.")

"We never settle at the first mediation"
("Did you know this is the second mediation?")

Let's move along to _always_, another word you often ignore. And, let's move immediately to translations.

"I always win my cases in front of Judge Jones."
("Does the other side know Judge Jones is on vacation next month?")

"I always get at least $500,000.00 to settle these kinds of cases."
("At least three years ago and before tort reform I did.")

"I always negotiate this way."
("Maybe that's why I can't get my cases settled")

"I always tell the truth."
("At least my version of the truth.")

Final usually has only one significant context for mediators. Many of you have to suppress a smile or your laughter after you hear final. Other variations of "final" include "bottom line", "best and final", "line drawn in the sand" (in Texas substitute dirt for sand), or as we also say in Texas our "fish or cut bait." All of these variations are followed by the word *offer*.

Good mediators really don't need to translate these words. These words, however, enjoy even less credibility depending upon the stage production surrounding their utterance.

You've been there. It's 5:00 P.M. This wonderful, older, but now cranky lawyer looks up at you and with venom in his voice and a steely eye says,

"They beat us down as far as we can go. You tell them that one million dollars is our final offer. We mean that. Don't come back with an offer less than one million dollars. We're not taking their last offer of $875,000.00. They're jerking us around. We've got to draw the line.

We are drawing the line. Now, you'll tell them every word I just said, won't you, Mr. Mediator?"
"Yes Jim, and with the same tone and enthusiasm."

(Twenty Minutes Later)
    "Jim, their next offer is $915,000.00."
    "Well, ok then, Mediator, tell them our next offer is $975,000.00."

I've never actually counted, but I'm sure I hear the words "win" and "lose" at least ten times during the course of a mediation. Lawyers, bless them, are especially fond of these two words. "Win" and "lose" are rarely defined when spoken. What does "winning" and "losing" mean exactly in the context of a dispute? And, who actually wins or loses? The parties? Their lawyers? Both? None? These two words, or so I think, are often used carelessly and thoughtlessly, rarely the product of objective risk assessment and usually to intimidate. Also, these two words set up the classic win –lose paradigm. I win.

You lose. Theses words suffocate the concept of a collaborative, creative negotiation and make win-win outcomes seem like science fiction.

Of course, winning and losing is most often used in terms of a predicted outcome before a judge, jury, appellate court or arbitrator. But, at best, such predictions are sheer guesses, sometimes bad ones. These guesses are thoughtless because nothing has more variables than our civil justice system. So many unknowns exist? Who will be the judge? Who will actually sit on a jury? What evidence will be admitted? How will a witness handle cross-examination? How will the jury react to the evidence and the witnesses? What will move an arbitrator? Will an appellate court really be interested in a case? And, most important, how will the parties and businesses cope until a true final outcome is reached? The costs, economic and emotional, are great.

For mediators, win and lose might be easy to ignore, except for the fact, due to television, film, and perception, these words seem real to parties unfamiliar with the unpredictability of our civil justice system.

Good lawyers don't truly believe these words because they appreciate uncertainty and risk. But, lawyers, to reel in and assure clients, often oversell a case. Mediators often hear a party say, "My lawyer never told me we could lose." Maybe the lawyer never said any such thing. Maybe there was no over selling. But, that's what the party wanted to hear or believe.

Despite bravado, arrogance, or just good solid advocacy lawyers will absolutely, positively never do one thing, i.e. sign a written warranty of outcome for a client. A defense lawyer who suggests there is no way a case may be lost will not sign a letter promising to return his fees if the case is lost. Similarly, a plaintiff's lawyer will not sign a written guarantee that the client will receive the $300,000.00 net on a settlement offer, even if the trial goes the wrong way.

As such, mediators might ignore the "win" word uttered by lawyer. But, the mediator must translate these words for the parties. Parenthetically, lawyers usually do not mind mediators doing so for a simple reason. I call it the Declining Curve of Credibility.

Ethical lawyers, and I believe the vast majority are ethical, tell clients what they need to hear. But, a client, if the lawyer's message is too strong, wonders whether the lawyer is really on his side. This phenomenon describes the Declining Curve of Credibility and explains one reason mediators exist. A mediator, because of her neutral role, may clearly, but not coercively, help a party appreciate risk and unpredictability in a way that a party's lawyer may not. A mediator is not predicting whether someone will win or someone will lose. A mediator, to simplify, is suggesting that no one really knows. Without such a translation, a party may not re-evaluate or make an informed decision.

The words "good faith" and "bad faith" have become more common language in mediation, although it is usually entirely unclear what the speaker means by these words. Because these words are used carelessly and imprecisely, mediators often ignore them or feel the need to translate them. These words usually arise in the following contexts.

(Lawyer to opposing party, during joint session)
> For the reasons I have just set out, we do not believe your case has any merit; but we are here to try to resolve this matter in good faith.

(Party or lawyer to the mediator in a private caucus)
> That's just a bad faith offer. The other side didn't come to this mediation in good faith.

In the first illustration, what does the lawyer really mean by the words good faith? The juxtaposition borders on the absurd. After twenty minutes of telling the party why his case is terrible, the lawyer promises his client is present not just in good faith; but, in <u>complete good faith</u>. What would you think if someone said that to you? Is the translation "Ignore everything I said first because we want to settle this dispute?" Or, is the translation, "I meant every word I said, but we have our own ideas about what constitutes a good faith settlement?" Regardless, these words are at the very least confusing, and at the very worst, lacking in credibility.

In the second illustration, the bad faith reference is easier to translate. The speaker is saying he didn't like the offer. The speaker is not saying what would have constituted a good faith offer. The second reference, not attending the mediation in good faith, probably means the other party is not doing what the speaking party wants them to do.

The interesting thing about good faith-bad faith jargon is that the complaining party has set no standard for his own conduct or analyzed whether he is acting in good faith or bad faith. My internal reaction to these words is they often constitute whining. My actual response to the use of these words is to ask questions.

> "What would a good faith proposal have been and why?"
> "If the other side made a good faith proposal as you have now defined it, what would be your good faith response?"
> If you think the other side's case is really so terrible, what motivates you to be at this mediation in complete good faith?"
> "What is good faith?"

"What is bad faith?"

"Describe your last good faith negotiation. What happened?"

"Bad faith to me means you really don't trust the other side's intentions. What worries you the most regarding their approach to this negotiation?"

"If I go back to the other side and they elect to make a good faith offer, will you pledge to make a good faith response?"

Of course, good faith and bad faith are entirely subjective and defined by a party's perception of fairness, outcome, and risk. But, the mediator as a teacher may ask the parties what they truly mean by these words and assist the parties in understanding that good faith is a two way street. You want good faith? You have to give good faith. You receive good faith. You have to respond in good faith. Good faith, if all parties truly understand it, means that the parties want a credible, constructive negotiation.

Another phrase that mediators hear frequently and do not favor is "we're wasting time." Usually, these comments are made somewhere between 2:00pm-4:00pm. "Wasting time" usually means that the negotiations are stalled or going too slowly. But, "wasting time," while it might reflect frustration and how a party is feeling, is often an objectively incorrect statement.

First, the dispute that brought the parties to mediation may have been raging for months and years and a great deal of time has likely already been wasted. Conflicts and disputes are rarely created in one day. Why should they be resolved in less than five hours? Eight to twelve hours of mediation pales in comparison to the weeks, months, and often years that lie ahead of the parties if the dispute is not resolved. And, the parties are assuming no responsibility for the fact that the slow pace of the process is due to their own stubbornness and intransigence.

I have come to look forward to the wasting time comment for two reasons. I suppose that I should say that all good mediators must always know how to turn any negative into a positive. That skill is part of the art of mediation. You begin to look forward to words that afford you the opportunity to teach, redirect, and inspire. Acknowledging feelings, even ones you think are a bit silly, is a powerful tool, if not a gift you may give to another human being.

To the party who has told you "we're wasting time," you have a number of possible approaches, each of which allows you to either acknowledge, teach, inspire, or redirect. Consider any of the following.

> "I know you are feeling frustrated, but this whole dispute has been frustrating to you, It's been a real long haul, and it will likely

go on for a great deal of time, if we do not resolve it now."

Or

"I realize this is going slower than you would like. I'm a little frustrated too. Is there anyway we might speed things up"?

Or

"We're all a bit frustrated. But, the road ahead is much longer. What can we do to make today go better? What would you suggest?"

All these approaches acknowledge frustration, remind the party of the time that lies ahead, and invite the parties to suggest ways to move the process along. Interestingly, a party will often suggest a good way to move the process along. And what better path could a mediator have than a path that a party suggests?

Many mediators dread hearing the "I" word- <u>impasse</u>. Of course, the mediator declares the impasse, but parties use the word <u>impasse</u> often.

Mediators simply may not live in fear of hearing the word <u>impasse</u>. But, beyond that, mediators must live for the moments of impasse. Impasse, real or imagined, is the moment a mediator earns her stripes. Overcoming and defeating impasse is the stuff from which legends are born. Truly great mediators somehow convert the impossible to the possible. Reputations are created from resolving a dispute that all thought was impossible to settle. People talk about mediators who settled the impossible, unsettleable case- not the easy ones everyone expected to resolve. The psychology and art of mediation is using the moment of perceived or real impasses as an energy source and develop the resolve not to quit when everyone else is ready to do so.

Summoning the requisite courage and resolve at such moments is not always easy. The hopelessness of the moment may suffocate a mediator's soul and the way is not often easy to find. But, there is almost always a way for those who are patient and true of heart. But, until that bright light goes on, you have a little light that will always go on.

The little light is the one that you shine on the others that tells them for whatever reason that you have faith and hope and are not ready to give up. Sometimes, that energy, if it is palpable and real, energizes everyone. New ideas surface. Hope is restored.

Finally, it's very late in the day and someone tells you "we're leaving." Bags are getting packed, briefcases are being closed, and laptops are being shut down. You believe, however, that things aren't really over.

At such moments, you have to summon up the great Motown song "Aint to Proud to Beg." Mediators may not be proud. And mediators, if they still believe, have to be willing to beg. Sometimes, begging at such moments is difficult to do. A part of you may actually, if you are honest, want everyone to leave. You want to go home. You want to get away. You did your best. If that's what they want – fine, just go. Begging almost seems cheap and demeaning. But, alas, you must.

You beg and plead for any time the party will give you. You may have to plead "Just give me fifteen minutes more." And, like your child, you may have to beg for fifteen more minutes after that. Of course, you may not falsely imprison parties. But, sometimes your pleas are honored and a short time later there is a resolution.

The words and phrases mediators often hear may become a source of consternation, or they may, if anticipated, become a source of energy and opportunity to lead and inspire.

Chapter 17

On Making a Living

"Don't ask about my business, Kay."
Michael in The Godfather

Much has been written and said about marketing a mediation or neutral practice.

I think it should be stated initially that creating and maintaining a mediation practice is a difficult and daily challenge. No one has to use a particular mediator in most instances. Mediators also labor under certain illusions about their relationship with the market they serve.

The greatest illusion is that people remember you. Many mediators believe, especially after an epic mediation in which they resolve a dispute which no one thought could ever be settled, that the parties and their counsel will remember them. Most of the time, unfortunately, this is not the case. On more than a few occasions, I have had the pleasure of lawyers or parties bragging about the valiant efforts of another mediator. I love to hear their stories because the success of our colleagues helps all mediators and boosts the reputation and image of mediation. But, after hearing such an amazing story told, I always want to know who the mediator was. Over ninety percent of the time, I swear, the person telling the story does not remember the mediator's name. I'm positive the mediator believed he/she would never be forgotten and would be broken-hearted to hear this story.

I have tried to figure out what exactly this means. Is it that the outcome was significant and the mediator's role is not remembered as significant? Remember, the story described a truly outstanding effort. Most people remember the name of the doctor who did especially good work. Is it that the mediation involved simply a one or two day relationship? But, the storyteller often describes what the mediator looked like and the specific way she dealt with a difficult problem. The mediator probably also believed the lawyer went back to his office and told all his partners about this heroic effort. Of course, a name would help. Business cards, coffee mugs, giveaways… do people really keep those things? Do you keep those things?

The reason that this problem is so terribly important is that mediators believe that every successful mediation creates four or five new mediations. I think that is true, if people remember the mediator's name. I know what you are thinking. That lawyer will check his file to remember your name. Wrong. Lawyers are crisis managers and usually respond to what is right in front of them.

So, is there a cure for the problem of the outstanding, invisible mediator? I think you understand we are talking about visibility. The problem is what to do about it.

Beyond business cards and coffee mugs, I have heard of other possible solutions. The most often discussed solutions include bar association speeches or writing articles. I think such things are in and of themselves good and worthwhile tasks. I just don't think they create visibility.

We know what you cannot do. You can't add to the "Spam" your market already receives or inundate your market with annoying, repetitive announcements. But, I do think there are some fundamental, basic things you can do which seem to work!

Step one is an appropriate thank you e-mail after a mediation. The e-mail thank you will be read and discarded. The e-mail should express a desire to work together again. Step two is to create a reminder to send another e-mail in three months. The second e-mail basically suggests you haven't seen Ms. X in three months and you would be happy to be of any assistance. The third step, and it is truly optional, is to create a newsletter and send that to your market on a quarterly basis.

The newsletter is not an advertisement. The

newsletter is educational, informative, and designed to teach your market how to better use the mediation process. The newsletter should be four pages or less, sent electronically, and offered no more than four times a year. The content should be valuable and unique.

As much as I dislike personal promotion and marketing, I have grudgingly come to the conclusion that the invisible mediator is a real problem.

The next illusion is that your market will be loyal to you. I apologize for being the bearer of bad news; but, your market, whatever you think it is, will not be loyal to you. In fact, your market will cheat on you all the time. The market is not faithful. Remember this.

The delicate psyche of a mediator believes something like this. I really bust my butt for Mr. Blue and all or most of Mr. Blue's cases get resolved. Mr. Blue thinks I'm wonderful (maybe Mr. Blue does think that). Mr. Blue would not possibly have any other mediator do his cases.

Sorry, chief. I saw Mr. Blue at Jane's mediation center. And, I hate to tell you this; but, Mr. Blue was mediating a case. I have the photographs to prove it. Looks like Mr. Blue likes Jane a lot. Notice the warm handshake. And, isn't this a settlement agreement? I know…it hurts. It hurts a lot.

How could Mr. Blue do this? I thought he would adjust his schedule to only use me? I thought he would insist other lawyers use me. Mr. Blue told me I was the very best mediator he ever had. I gave Mr. Blue's cases everything…and now, he's seeing Jane.

Sometimes, if you are being honest and hopefully also laughing, it almost feels this way. Of course, scheduling, the preferences of others and the type of case explains why Mr. Blue uses other mediators. But, you say, you guessed Mr. Blue was cheating on you. It still hurts. Effort, sacrifice, good work, fairness, and professionalism almost always create loyalty. But, is there some outside the box explanation, beyond scheduling and the preferences of others, that explains Mr. Blue's behaviors. I hope you are sitting down. I will offer two theories to explain Mr. Blue's infidelity. I am quite certain you will like neither of them.

We're talking about relationships, aren't we? Have you ever thought about your relationship with counsel you mediate with frequently? These are relationships born of trust and overcoming huge, sometimes insurmountable, obstacles. The relationship may be safely described as intimate.

Intimacy involves many things; but, it almost always involves a terribly honest communication between two people. These two people come to know each other very, very well.

Familiarity, knowing someone exceeding well, may be a very, very good thing in certain contexts. In a relationship between a mediator and an attorney, familiarity may also be a very, very good thing. You may cut through a lot of brush quickly. Both people know how each other thinks. But, could this familiarity ever be a bad thing in a mediation context?

Think about those people with whom you truly enjoy an intimate relationship. Think about the people you truly, truly know and the people who really know you. You know when such people are telling you the truth and when they are not. You know how to read these people. You see beyond the words and the denials. These people know you know them.

In the context of mediation, this level of awareness and intimacy may also be a bad thing. You see, Mr. Blue ultimately realizes he cannot mislead you or misdirect you or manipulate you. Mr. Blue believes you will see right through it. Using a purely economic illustration, Mr. Blue believes that he might be able to convince Jane he really needs $400,000 to settle a case when he only really needs $300,000. Mr. Blue wants to take a shot at getting the extra $100,000 or close to it. Jane affords Mr. Blue at least the chance to achieve that goal. In summary, I am describing the curse of knowing someone too well. More cynically stated, most participants in a mediation want to able to hold something back from the mediator.

The second theory to explain Mr. Blue's infidelity is that your "act," no matter how effective, becomes stale and predictable over time. I told you wouldn't like this and maybe you don't want to believe it.

Over time, Mr. Blue begins to understand how you think and what you do. Mr. Blue almost knows what you are going to say before you say it. And, as with all relationships, what started out as exciting becomes predictable, boring and even annoying. In this regard, please read the essay _On Change and Reinvention_.

The bottom line is the relationship between a mediator and an attorney is like any other relationship. The relationship begins, develops, matures, improves; but, over time, if you are not careful, the relationship may deteriorate.

The final illusion that impedes the development of a neutral's practice is the pretense (lie) that a mediator is too busy. Many mediators would like the world to believe that they are fully booked three or four months ahead. For a very, very few, such a statement may be true. But, for most mediators, keeping their calendars reasonably full is a challenge.

Why do some mediators lie about this? I suppose mediators wish to create the image of success. Mediators do not wish to appear vulnerable or needy. Mediators do not want to acknowledge that their practices, like everyone else's, go through up and down cycles. Mediators do not want to admit, even after five, ten, or twenty years of practice, that they count each mediation and thank the stars that they are busy or that a month has been a good one.

I don't want this to sound like an AA meeting; but, I feel a profound sense of obligation. After sixteen years as a mediator, I count each mediation. I am appreciative of any piece of work that falls my way. I know that I do a very, very good job but I worry that the next month could be my last or that the bottom might fall out. I worry that I might wake up and not be doing what I truly love to do. I am, in sum, just like most of you. Now don't we all feel better?

I think much of this concern relates to how truly much we like what we do. For most of us, mediation is a passion, a calling, something that we know is a very worthy and noble pursuit. Sometimes, despite longevity and success rates, we worry that events beyond our control could invalidate years of struggle and effort. Some mediators have told me that they feel they are only as good as their last mediation. I think that is a terrible thing to feel.

I do not know how to fully alleviate this anxiety; but, acknowledgement is always a good beginning. I do think, as I have suggested in other essays, that mediators have to trust other mediators more. If a group of ten or twenty mediators meet quarterly, and if they were willing to be honest, the expression of these concerns could be therapeutic. Beyond emotional relief, mediators should realize that ten or twenty heads are better than one. A mediator looks at her small corner of a very large universe. Collectively, mediators who share see trends and may identify patterns that are susceptible of being corrected. Sometimes, small adjustments bring back the market.

I also think mediators may be more competitive and territorial than they wish to admit. Maybe a mediator worries that giving away a marketing strategy or concept will result in a loss of business instead of believing that sharing may provide greater returns for everyone. In many ways, mediators do not behave in the way they instruct others to behave.

I suppose, in the end, I hold onto this simple belief. The goal of any mediator, beyond developing his art, is to be part of an outstanding community of mediators. The market will value mediation because the mediation community practices it well, effectively, and professionally. Such quality will sustain the market for mediation services and should provide a community of mediators with abundant work to do.

Chapter 18

On Staying Well
and Avoiding Burnout

"Stayin' alive, stayin' alive"
Stayin' Alive,
Barry Gibb, Maurice Gibb, and Robin Gibb

Some addictions are bad for you. Other addictions are harmless and may even be a source of great joy. Mediation may become an addiction too.

What is addictive about mediation? I think, plain and simple, it is the unquenchable passion to help people resolve difficult, often terrible disputes. I think every successful mediator very much feels this passion and feels that they are privileged to do the work that mediators do. Mediation is much more of a calling than a "job." Mediators are driven by the spiritual rewards their calling brings them and not money. Many mediators feel, yours truly included, that is amazing that they get paid to do the work they so truly love.

While I am a devoted runner, I do not experience the promised "runners' high." The best part of my daily run is seeing my home in the distance as I am returning. But, I have experienced the "mediator's high" many, many times. You no doubt know this feeling. The "mediator's high" usually occurs at the moment of resolution. You feel the pervasive sense of relief of the parties. You see the difference in their faces and in their eyes. You get the strong feeling, despite all the cynicism and conflict in the world, that people are truly amazing. You see their strength and courage in resolving sometimes unimaginable problems. You often see the great talent and professionalism of the lawyers who participate in the process.

And, you are in awe of the process. How did a dispute that no one thought could ever resolve actually settle? Even if you've mediated hundreds or thousands of times, you are never any less amazed by the sheer magic of a process that is beyond definition and which seems to reinvent itself and surprise you.

This is also the moment <u>the mediator</u> lets go. Each of you would have your own way of describing this. For me, it is the moment that all the extra weight I have been gladly and willingly carrying is taken off my shoulders. I feel it in my body. And then, if it's also the same for you, I feel it in my soul. Every detail, fact, feeling, number, or emotion that I have captured in my brain simply leaves. My mind turns to mush at the end of a mediation.

I also have noticed that I really can't (or don't want to) listen to anything at the conclusion of a mediation. Mediators violate the theory of primacy on a daily basis. We actively listen to over 90% of the content, instead of less than 15%. In some ways, such continuous active listening is unnatural. At the very least, such active listening is exhausting. You either want silence or you gravitate towards noise to block out other sounds. Led Zeppelin or Bruce Springsteen at high decibel levels in my car does the trick for me.

As with any other high, you need to come down from it. But, as you are coming down, you find yourself thinking about tomorrow's mediation because you hope for the high to return. You see, dear readers, why mediation may well become an addiction.

We know the favorable aspects of this addiction. But, over time, could this passion and addiction be bad for you? We do not have any reliable studies in this regard. But, in an earlier published article, I pondered who takes care of the caretakers?

Most mediators are caretakers, spending most of their professional lives helping others. I have written about the loneliness mediators experience in this book. But, another side effect of mediation practice is the very human need to get back on a personal level what you so willingly give to others.

As with other professions, mediators need time away from their passion and addiction. "Time away" does not simply mean an annual vacation; but, those are very good, too. "Time away" also means a few days each month when you are doing something other than mediating disputes. Maybe you want to teach mediation, adopt a peer mediation program, write about dispute resolution, or just do some gardening or take in a movie. Whatever it is you like that takes you away from mediating disputes, you just do it. I know this is the most preachy writing in this book; but, just take this time for yourself and be good to yourself. If you have an obsessive-compulsive tendency and you can't do it for yourself, do it for those you serve and try to help. Your audience needs you fresh and energized.

I think of it this way. My "Friday" group expects the same level of energy as my "Monday" group and should not be concerned with what I did the rest of the week. Mediators know there are no "routine" or "simple" cases. Mediators must bring their "A game" every day. And, we've established I hope that mediation is exhausting work on many levels. A mediator may never be thinking privately "How am I going to get through this one today?" And, it's only Wednesday.

Unbelievably, the passion which came so quickly may be lost if a mediator does not develop a more mature relationship with the process.

Lawyers often report to me that a mediator in another city is burned-out, doesn't seem to care, or has lost their tenacity. If too many lawyers begin to feel this way, a mediator may be in danger of losing his practice. I realize it's very difficult when one is just beginning to mediate or their practice is going very well to believe that there are dangers lurking up ahead.

But, a mediator's passion should and must convert to love and respect for the process so that the relationship may grow and prosper for a very long time. Removing yourself consistently from the world of conflict is good both for the mediator and the parties she so zealously serves.

Another problem, and it is certainly ironic, is that mediators give so much to strangers that they find the may not give as much to those they love and those who depend on them. The very last thing a mediator wants after a very difficult, vexing day is a problem or conflict at home. Also, listening to those you love may become a problem. How many of you after ten hours of active listening have had a spouse, a significant other, a child or a friend accuse you of not listening or paying attention?

Of course, you are not listening and you may be incapable of listening very well. But, is that fair for your significant other? And, what is fair for you?

I have to confirm that I have not always handled this problem very well. The best I have come up with is giving myself thirty minutes to "decompress" after a mediation. I have come to accept that after a mediation I need a brief time not to be around anyone. I need to stare at Peace Lake by my office. Or go for a walk. Or, watch television...anything which does not require human interaction or in which I am being asked to do anything. I used to worry that twenty or thirty minutes was "selfish" time. Now I believe it is simply an occupational necessity. Something I need to do for myself. And, something I need to do for those I love so that I may be attentive and available to them. I'm certain you will think of a better word than "decompression;" but, for me, it best describes this feeling.

Finally, I ponder whether mediators, because of the caretaking they do, become more needy. If you spend your life paying so much attention to others, do you occasionally wish someone would pay that much attention to you? And, do you ever get disappointed if that does not happen at the very moment you need it? Do you ever expect others to be as aware of you as you are to the total strangers you serve?

You probably have guessed that your faithful writer has felt these demons from time to time. The first part of any cure is to acknowledge such feelings exist. With time, especially as you develop a balance with your relationship with the process, those feelings seem to lessen. I think (hope) mediators begin to realize that as caretakers they unconditionally offer the gift of the process to people who desperately need it. In the end, you receive more back than you ever give. You simply begin to feel very blessed and fortunate.

As you might also guess, I have deep affection and admiration for those who take up the cause of peace on a daily basis. I suppose the intent of this essay is to say, in an affectionate way, take good care of yourselves. In a highly conflicted would, we need as many peacemakers as we can get and we need you around for a very long time.

Chapter 19

On Peer Mediation

"Teach your children well"
Teach Your Children, Crosby, Stills, Nash & Young

I include an essay on peer mediation because my experiences with it provide me hope in a world on the brink. I also include this essay because I believe that peer mediation in many ways helps realize the true potential of the modern mediation movement.

Conflict resolution and peacemaking is a process susceptible of being taught and also being learned. The evidence of conflict, including in our schools, is overwhelming. We must make a societal and cultural shift to instruct all children in conflict resolution techniques and skills. We owe it to our children to do so because they will live in a far better world. Realizing this goal should be a priority of every mediation group and every mediation association. If every mediator adopted a school and taught a peer mediation class, we would be making good progress. Alternatively, mediation associations should be lobbying legislatures to fund and institutionalize such training. Peacemaking and constructive dispute resolution should become the first option for our children. Achieving such a goal could be our finest legacy.

The question you must ask yourself is how much better would this world be if every child had some instruction in conflict resolution? We have to believe passionately that our world would be a better place. Children, by nature and as is their birthright, are hopeful and optimistic. Children are generally collaborative and cooperative. Children are also competitive. A dispute over who gets the last swing at the playground does not have to end badly. Does one child get the swing and win? Does one child not get the swing and lose? Does it boil down to who is the most powerful and the quickest? And, does anyone truly win and will there be reprisal later? Or, is there a process that allows for a win-win situation?

Perhaps one of the most troubling aspects of our world is that cynicism abounds. Of course the dire conflicts that beset our planet inspire such negativity and pessimism. Many people believe that "win-win" outcomes are the stuff of fairy tales. But, fortunately, children are not so jaded and may learn and accept a process which provides good outcomes for everyone. Children have a tendency to want to help and assist others. And, children cherish being empowered to do the right thing. But, as with everything else, children need guidance, instruction, and direction.

Children, who later become adults, do not inherently posses complex problem solving skills. Children learn about conflict and how conflicts are resolved in a number of ways, many of which result in an ostensible "winner" and an ostensible "loser."

For example, children learn about conflict and conflict resolution from their parents and their interaction with their siblings. Or, children can learn such things from their interactions with their peers. Children also learn about conflict from television and movies. Children may even learn about conflict by playing or observing sports, which is an organized, structured form of conflict.

What exactly do children learn about conflict from these sources? Some children may begin to believe conflict is terrible; i.e. observing a horrible fight between their parents. Some children may believe conflict is good; i.e. "I grabbed the ball from Jimmy and really showed him." Many children, at a frighteningly young age, believe from their experiences with conflict that there are winners and losers. Of course, primal instincts create two obvious options for dealing with conflict; i.e. fight or flight. A child may see her mother always walking away from conflict and conclude such technique must be good. Or, a child may see an older brother exert his power over a friend and get his way and that must be good.

Without indicting the media, television and film frequently glorify power, might, and strength and even glorify such concepts as revenge and getting even. In a school setting, conflicts fester and escalate, often with a resultant fight producing an ostensible winner and loser. More often than not, the conflict is not resolved fully and triggers a series of future conflicts and fights.

Conflict resolution skills provide an alternative to fight or flight and if properly integrated in the hearts and minds of children, may become the preferred method of resolving disputes.

Most disputes which arise in schools are a result of poor, dysfunctional communication. If you ask a principal or teacher at any school what is the source of most conflicts at school, the principal will advise you that rumors or "he said-she said" are the source of most eruptions. Many fights involve two students who have never spoken directly to each other about the specific issue, but who have heard things from others that have angered them.

Such disputes are almost always resolvable through peer mediation. Fellow students, trained in conflict resolution, fully understand the nature of such disputes and may direct their peers to more peaceful paths. Also, once students resolve their disputes and sign an agreement, students tend to honor the written pact they sign. And, students who have had successful mediation experiences tell others and may then wish to learn such skills themselves.

Another fascinating impact of such training on students is that it upgrades self-esteem, provides leadership skills, and often even translates into improved academic success. Interestingly, students who receive conflict resolution training often bring their talents home to their communities.

My favorite story in this regard involves a seventh grader, Mandy, who I had the honor to teach. Mandy was exceptionally bright, but small in stature and usually quiet. On a Saturday morning, Mandy's parents had a terrible fight. Mandy instructed her parents to sit down and she was going to help them mediate their dispute. Two hours later, Mandy facilitated a resolution of her parents' dispute. Mandy's mom and dad were about to get up from the table when Mandy advised them the process was not completed until their agreement was written up and signed. Thirty minutes later, Mandy taped her parents signed agreement to the refrigerator so no one would forget the resolution.

As Mandy reported this story to the class, I had to almost restrain tears. Mandy was so obviously proud of what she had done and the class erupted in applause for their colleague.

Mandy's story, although it's now over fifteen years old, remains with me as a shining light and exemple of the value and potential of providing our children with conflict resolution skills. When I think of Mandy's story, I imagine thousands and thousands of Mandy's and their impact at school, at home, in their communities, and as world leaders. I imagine a new generation of adults who believe that resolving disputes peaceably and constructively should always be the first resort.

I have never seen such instruction as a panacea; but, I do believe it is a significant step in the right direction towards a more peaceful world. I also believe mediators are in a unique and powerful position to lead this charge, as a way of giving something back to their communities and also in a very real way to support their philosophical belief and commitment to the process.

One final word on this topic. Should you read this, adopt a school, and teach a class, you will receive so much more back than you may possibly give. And, these students will inspire you. Many of these students come from situations you may hardly imagine. But, their strength, their wisdom, their desire to do right, and their hope is simply awe inspiring. Teaching such a class will create boundless ripples which go in directions you would never imagine.

Chapter 20

On Faith & Hope

"There's just not enough love in the world"
Not Enough Love in The World, Don Henley

(Special Thanks to the Strauss Institute at Pepperdine, my colleagues and students who inspired me to write this, and very special thanks to my new band-mates, "Steven Stills" and "Graham Nash" who provided the new music. I guess that makes me "Crosby").

For the final day of the advanced mediation training, I very much wanted to say something to the forty brilliant mediators who had come to learn from us and who, as always is the case, taught us so much more. I was also inspired by the evening before. The Strauss Institute hosted a faculty dinner for the great mediation scholars and experts from around the country who were teaching their summer skills courses. As I looked around the room, I wondered what I was doing there. So many of the people who had pioneered and profoundly impacted the modern mediation movement were present. The conversations were intoxicating, warm, and evidence of the greatness of the speakers. I went outside to drink it all in and I had a vision. I had also come to Pepperdine hoping to write this essay, one of the final installments of this book. I had struggled to get the words right and had tossed away four or five first efforts. But, sitting outside on a beautiful Malibu evening and still in the aura of these wonderful people, I realized that the words had not come because I was afraid, albeit unknowingly, to write them. I was afraid of being maudlin and of expressing sentiment. But, the inspiration and comfort of my colleagues restored my confidence and trust. I knew what I wanted to tell my class. And, I knew what I wanted to tell you.

I kept hearing the song "Easy To Be Hard" in my head as I was sitting outside. You remember how the song opens.

> "How can people be so heartless?
> How can people be so cruel?
> Is it easy to be hard?"

I think the song came to me because, despite being a cup half full person, I have felt my soul crushed by the heartless conflict, terror, and violence in our world. Beyond the terrible violence, the conflict has

seemingly suffocated our ability to express sentiment and show our hearts. Maybe now, especially
now, we need to show our hearts more than ever.

I remember as a child doing the duck and cover
drills, as if my wooden desk would save me if the
Soviet Union dropped nuclear bombs in New York
City some forty-five miles away. I used to wake up,
bathed in sweat, from the same recurrent nightmare. An emergency alert would come on our black
and white television. The bombs would land in one
hour. My family runs to the car and begins to drive.
But where? And, in minutes, the traffic is backed up
for miles. We all just wait in our cars. My mother is
crying. My father is angry. I reach over and hold my
brother as the bombs go off. Then, I would wake up,
usually screaming.

But, somehow sanity prevailed and the bombs
never fell. I became a high school student again, de-
tached from reason and reality, believing in writing
and poetry and thinking maybe I would fall in love
some day.

Plainfield, New Jersey was an eclectic, diverse,
racially mixed sleepy bedroom community of about
40,000 people. I had Italian, African American, Catholic, Protestant, and Jewish mothers. For high school
boys, playing ball was the common denominator.
The public park, which bordered my back yard, was
the meeting place for those who could hit a baseball
or shoot a basketball. Your race, ethnicity, or religion

mattered not. During summers, we would play from dusk to dawn. Probably the highest praise I received in high school was Clarence Jones telling me I could play ball-not becoming valedictorian. We did more than play ball. We became friends- good friends.

Then, one hot summer night in 1968, everything changed. Race riots were exploding around the United States. A riot had occurred three days earlier and just thirty miles away in Newark, New Jersey.

A rookie Plainfield police officer received an emergency call this hot summer night. Three hoods from the neighboring high school had driven their car into a predominantly African American part of town and had begun screaming racial epithets and threats at the top of their lungs. Suddenly, the hoods' car ran out of gas. An angry crowd had already gathered. The hoods took off running, with the crowd in tow. Someone called the police. The rookie police officer, with no back up or experience, got out of his car and started running towards the scene. The three hoods ran past him, but the crowd kept coming. The police officer fired two shots in the air, but the crowd did not stop. The rookie then fired into the crowd, hitting a twelve year old boy. The crowd engulfed the police officer and beat him to death.

And then, my quiet, safe hometown exploded. I could hear the gunshots from my backyard and I heard them night after night for weeks. Blockades were erected. The National Guard was called in and remained for months.

The park, our meeting ground, became a no man's land. Blockades and patrols prevented access. Everyone was afraid. Doors needed extra locks. You watched where you went. Grass grew over the infield in the park. No new basketball nets were put up. And, I never saw Clarence again.

Of course, we also had Vietnam. Back then, in high school, we didn't really know what it was all about, or even where Vietnam actually was. But, we did come to understand what war could do to people.

Mr. McMahon was our favorite 9th grade English teacher and also our basketball coach. During the 10th grade we were advised that Mr. McMahon was drafted and had been sent to Vietnam. We had seen our share of movies and figured coach would come back as a war hero. Coach was an interesting combination. He was in love with poetry and would read to us with such passion that most of us began, however covertly, to enjoy and read poetry. But, Mr. McMahon was one tough coach. We loved him as a coach, but slacking off was simply not tolerated.

In the early winter of 1969, we began our final varsity basketball season. We had been together for a while, played excellent defense, had two real shooters, and had become an outstanding team. We started the season with Coach Grant, but were told Coach McMahon would return and coach us by mid-season. By the time Coach McMahon walked into practice that cold dreary February day, we were 12-1, including a 20-point victory over our archrival, Montclair.

Coach seemed pretty much the same to us. Of course, we were seniors, full of ourselves, and saw what we wanted to see. We noticed coach didn't laugh as much and there were far fewer jokes. He threw a blackboard at Jimmy Thomas; but, Jimmy deserved it, and we all threw stuff at him.

We thought a monkey could probably coach us. We were that good. We cruised through the rest of the season unbeaten. We were 21-1 heading into our final game, a rematch with Montclair, who we had thrashed earlier in the season.

We were required to go to the Chapel room for pre-game. We actually liked it. The room had those old hinged, wooden desks, the kind you could put stuff in. We liked the desks because you could pick up the top, slam it down, and make a lot of noise.

As Coach McMahon walked in, we were already slamming the desks.

"Do you want to win this game?" Coach yelled.

"Yes, Coach, we want to win," we screamed back as we banged on our desks.

"How bad do you want it?" asked Coach.

"We want it bad," we responded as we banged away.

"How bad?" Coach barked.

"Real, real bad," we yelled back. We did not stop banging.

"Do you know how bad I want it?" Coach asked.

"How bad Coach?" we responded above the angry drumbeat of our desks.

"I want it as bad as I wanted that first gook to flip in my sights," Coach shrieked.

And then, the desk drumbeat stopped. No one made a sound. The room fell quiet. It was as if the air was sucked out of the room. Coach led us out and we lost our final game by 14 points. Two months later, before school was over, Coach didn't show up one day. We graduated and received our four-year college deferral.

Within the first eight weeks of my freshman year at Duke, two things happened. The first thing was the draft lottery. Lotteries mean something different today; but, in 1969 we trundled into a large room to hear the news together. The conventional wisdom was that if your draft number was 200 or better, you would probably not be drafted after college and if the war was still on. Anything under 100 was a death sentence. I drew number 37. I think it was the only time in college I wished I smoked dope. Beer did well that night and I drank a lot of beer.

One month later, campus organizers were encouraging students to sign up for the march on Washington D.C. Two weeks later, twenty busses left Durham, North Carolina, heading north.

I was on one of those busses, wearing a real army jacket my roommate had given me. I thought it seemed appropriate and looked cool. The whole bus ride the organizers advised us what to do if we were "harassed by pigs" or "gassed". By the time we were left off at Arlington Cemetery, I had reached the apex of paranoia. I remember as the name of a deceased American soldier was placed around my neck wondering what this walk might be like. I also felt the weight of the soldier's name. Maybe for the first time I realized people were actually dying in Vietnam. We were to place our nametags in caskets in front of the U.S Capitol. About a mile from the Capitol, a burly D.C. police officer pulled me out of the line. I remember feeling terrified immediately.

"Your gonna get in trouble kid," said the officer.

"For what sir?" I asked.

"It's your jacket, kid," the officer said.

"What's wrong with it?" I asked.

"It's a real army jacket. They're busting people up ahead for wearing them, kid," said the officer.

I think the officer could see my panic. I didn't know what to do. He reached toward my coat and removed the very large peace button that I was wearing. He gently folded the pocket over the military designation and stuck it together with the peace button.

"You're good to go now kid," the officer said. I breathed an expression of thanks, got back in line and dropped my soldiers name in the casket.

Later that night in a church basement waiting for our busses home, two tear gas canisters were accidentally thrown through the church basement windows. Frightened, exhausted, and with our eyes stinging, we felt we had managed our escape. But, we also knew more grave, more frightening dangers lay ahead.

Six months before I graduated, the war ended and the draft was over. I could go to law school. We would never see a world like this again; or so I thought.

I was so utterly naïve. I believed that the world would finally learn from the painful lessons of the past. I also believed that my children, if I was ever fortunate to have children, would live in a safer, more secure, less violent world.

I flash back to these times and events often. I flashed back to them on this night in Malibu. I thought we would have a better world; but, the world is even more precarious and inhumane. I often ask myself "Is this really our world? How does someone live in this world?"

I thought about this as I was about to address these wonderful mediators. I also realized that I had many hopes for them, hopes I prayed I could express and maybe we might still believe in.

So, for a few minutes close you eyes and open your hearts.

We have faith and hope that the modern mediation movement is about something greater than we truly understand today.

We have faith and hope that as peacemakers and teachers of peacemakers we are casting stones in the water creating ripples that will flow into the mighty currents of peace.

We have faith and hope in people and believe in human beings' sense of goodness and grace and love.

We have faith and hope that we will recognize and appreciate diversity as our greatest strength and that our world shall one day respect and nurture its differences.

We have faith and hope that we will teach our children peacemaking and that they as parents will teach their children.

We have faith and hope that as mediators and peacemakers we make a difference and that we shall have the hunger, strength, and persistence to continue to do so.

We have faith and hope in the mediation process, a magical gift we are only beginning to understand and shall never fully understand.

We have faith and hope in each other as part of the order of peacemakers and make a commitment to being good friends and taking care of each other.

Beyond anything else, we have faith and hope. We must always have faith and hope.

I began writing this essay by the blue Pacific and completed it by Peace Lake.

May your hearts and lives always have peace and bless you for the gifts and kindness that you self-lessly and thoughtfully give to so many.

Chapter 21

On Ripples from Peace Lake

"Sky of love, sky of tears (a dream of life),
sky of glory and sadness (a dream of life),
sky of mercy, sky of fear (a dream of life)"
The Rising, Bruce Springsteen

"I can't believe the news today oh
I can't close my eyes and make it go away"
Sunday Bloody Sunday, U2

I draw strength from this lake by my mediation center; but, for many years I did not know why. I have always called it Peace Lake. It's actually Lake Austin; but I named it Peace Lake the day we moved in.

I see Peace Lake in the early morning when the sun makes it sparkle and glisten. I see her during the day as the many boats set sail. And, I have seen Peace Lake as the moon works her divine magic spell over her waters. I am drawn to Peace Lake during the many difficult moments of a mediation.

She seems to calm the often tortured souls of the disputants and she provides me with an unrelenting sense of hope.

I remember the day I truly fell in love with her and I know why. It was September 11th, the day we refer to now as only 911.

The day began like any other day. I retrieved my morning caffeine from ever dependable Mozart's. Mediations were supposed to happen. Lawyers and parties were supposed to be flying in. Resolutions were supposed to be reached. The authors who write their new books on laptops on our deck were present. All the usual suspects were where they always were. Peace Lake, as always, sparkled and shined.

Then, everything changed. The television showed the horrible pictures, strangers began to cry, and the skies became eerily silent. The tragedy which continued to unfold, live in front of our eyes, became more surreal and more unbearable to watch. What was happening? Why was it happening? How could this happen in this world? What kind of world is this? Is this the world we live in? And, the horror... the horror. What about the people? Fathers, mothers, sisters, brothers, sons, daughters, grandsons, granddaughters, just people. Human Beings. Like you. Like me. The sheer terror. The insanity of it all. Incomprehensible. This can't be happening...in this world...an allegedly civilized world.

People on the deck crying for help. Loved ones

in New York City. Loved ones on air planes. Crying because of the sheer loss. Crying just to be held. Crying to believe that this world could not be such a place. Make this a terrible dream we will wake up from. So that people do not hurt. So that people do not bleed. So that people do not die. So that people find their fathers, their mothers, their sisters, their brothers, even their children.

And, then.

Powerlessness and fear gives birth to anger and rage and a burning desire for revenge. I am clenching my fists. I want to break a window…something…anything. I want buildings somewhere else to fall. I want someone else to bleed. I want someone else to die. An eye for and eye. A tooth for a tooth. Balance will only be restored if there is payback! For the first time in my life I want to hurt somebody so badly I can almost taste it in my mouth and feel it in my heart. This is a terrible world. There is only one way to protect those I love.

But, then, Peace Lake called me. I threw stones angrily into her. I wanted to tear her waters apart. She is a myth. A careless name I gave her out of some sense of misguided hope and optimism. I was not a child when I named her. I was fifty. I should have known better.

It was my pathetic sentimental child calling to me. She was not real. She was my secret wish that I had made when I was eight years old-when I felt powerless, terrified, but still full of wishes and when I still believed. So delusional to still hope, to not have grown up to realize that the true sources of night terrors are real- they only take different forms. Monsters don't lurk under bed. But, they exist. And, they are human.

But, my stones don't tear Peace Lake apart. I want her waters to go black and dry up; but, instead she accepts these angry missiles lovingly and without reservation. She accepts my malevolent being, yet she does not grow dark. She does what she always does.

She takes my angry stones and a ripple forms. And one ripple creates another. And yet another. As each ripple creates a mother which gives birth to father and then a daughter and then a son I finally understand why I love her so much, why I am linked to her, why I draw strength, and why, even now, of all days, I feel hope. Because what we do somehow flows into her waters and goes someplace…where, we do not know. But we do not need to know.

I love her because the hearts, souls, minds, hopes, prayers and dreams of so many are contained in her waters. We each see her differently. We all believe in different things. But, we all hope. Hope that we are not powerless. And have faith. Faith that even the most small heart stones ripple and flow in some way that we don't understand. That the journey has a beginning, a middle, and ends somewhere.

Somewhere good.

Somewhere where every child is safe.

Somewhere where all people are respected.

Somewhere where our differences are our collective strengths.

Somewhere where sentiment, heart, belief, faith, and caring are the most powerful.

Somewhere where mistakes are acknowledged as human and forgiveness is always granted.

Somewhere where hope is embraced and not condemned as idealistic or immature.

Somewhere that peace exists as a potential for this world, one world, our children.

So now you know. And I am not ashamed. Or even embarrassed. I throw a stone each day in Peace Lake and make a wish and I do have hope.

Each stone in Peace Lake creates ripples that go somewhere I do not understand. No compass or map will help. But, I do know this. These ripples go somewhere wonderful, somewhere good, and somewhere warm. Peace Lake belongs to everyone.

Including you.

ISBN 1-41204638-6

9 781412 046381